THE LEGAL LAMPOON

THE LEGAL LAMPOON

◆

A Practical, no-nonsense Guide for anyone interested in becoming or hiring a lawyer

Richard T. Icci, J.D.

iUniverse, Inc.
New York Lincoln Shanghai

THE LEGAL LAMPOON
A Practical, no-nonsense Guide for anyone interested in becoming or hiring a lawyer

iUniverse books may be ordered through booksellers or by contacting:

iUniverse
2021 Pine Lake Road, Suite 100
Lincoln, NE 68512
www.iuniverse.com
1-800-Authors (1-800-288-4677)

Because of the dynamic nature of the Internet, any Web addresses or links contained in this book may have changed since publication and may no longer be valid.

ISBN: 978-0-595-45231-6 (pbk)
ISBN: 978-0-595-69310-8 (cloth)
ISBN: 978-0-595-89539-7 (ebk)

Printed in the United States of America

Dedicated to M.M. Rowan, without whose assistance this book would have remained a manuscript.

Contents

Preface

I am Richard T. Icci, J.D. The "J.D." stands for "Juris Doctor", which nowadays, is the coveted degree awarded by law schools to their graduates. At one time, law schools awarded a different distinction upon graduation (the "LL.B." degree), but those in higher places thought the "J.D." designation sounded more scholarly and carried more clout in today's World. A slightly post-Baby Boomer; I am now described as a member of "Generation X". I reside in Fairfield, Connecticut with my long-suffering wife of seventeen years and two sons; neither of whom will be encouraged to become attorneys.

Since 1986, when I began my career I have been engaged in trench warfare in the courts of both New York State and Connecticut. I have worked in the corporate legal department of a major Fortune 500 corporation and as a litigation attorney at one of the largest law firms in the country based in New York City. While working at a mid-sized firm, a small firm, in a partnership and, as a sole practitioner for the last fifteen years, I personally litigated cases in the five Boroughs of New York City, as well as many of the counties of New York outside the City.

Currently I handle what are referred to as "civil litigations" or "civil lawsuits" (these are cases of a non-criminal nature) primarily in the courts of the State of New York. To date, I have handled in excess of one thousand such cases, representing both claimants (plaintiffs) and defendants. My work has included dozens of trials and appeals. As a sole practitioner every aspect of my cases is handled by me; from preparing all of the necessary paperwork, to making all the court appearances and dealing exclusively with my clients. Consequently, the buck starts and stops with me.

I have written this book to demonstrate something sorely lacking in the press, on the big screen and on the television: that the truth about the legal profession is stranger and more comical than the fiction. Whether it is maniacal adversaries, illiterate foes, idiotic and crooked judges, egotistical clerics, certifiably insane clients or simply the run-of-the-mill irrational clients; the legal profession is a fertile breeding ground for comedy and should be viewed as such.

I will have achieved my purpose if I convince you that our system of "justice" is concerned with anything but achieving a just result; that our system of justice is not, and never was, meant to be taken seriously; and convince those of you who thought you would become instant millionaires upon graduation from law school, to save your money, as well as your sanity, and to pursue some other career and to convince those of you who were going to hire a lawyer to look a good deal more carefully into the individual you seek to retain.

Have I begun to scare you, young energetic hopefuls away yet? This is not my intent, but there are certain truths that one should be aware of before making the lifetime decision to enter the legal profession.

1

Extraordinary Wealth and Other Fairy Tales

The most significant reason why people enter the legal profession is their belief that all lawyers are wealthy. I can't say I blame them. Given the choice between wealth and poverty, most rational people would certainly choose wealth. An old attorney friend of mine kept a photograph of himself on his desk. In it he was standing in front of a Rolls Royce holding a champagne glass in his hand; a sign on the picture frame read—"poverty sucks".

It is true. Poverty does suck. But, does becoming an attorney automatically equate with wealth? Unfortunately, the answer is sometimes yes ... and sometimes no. Come along for the ride and see.

The largest influx of lawyers in this country has clearly come from the generations known as the "Baby Boomers" and "Generation X". The Baby Boomers have alternately been defined as children born of the World War II veterans, Korean War veterans, or children born during a certain time period, usually expressed as between the late 1940's and the early 1960's. Sometimes an odd statistical group of its own, or a sub-group of the Baby-Boomers, has been identified as "Generation X", or "Gen X". I, myself, seem to fall within the category of Generation X. These people don't quite fit into the Baby Boomer category, but they are also too old to be the Baby Boomers' children. The people of this Generation were born between the late 1950's to the mid-1960's and even late 1960's.

Simply put, if you are now approximately fifty to sixty years of age, you are a classic Baby Boomer. If you are now in your early to mid-forties, you are clearly in the Generation X category. I like to relate life to music. If you live for the music of the Beatles, the Rolling Stones and John Fogarty, you are most likely a Baby Boomer. If you prefer Elton John, Duran Duran and U-2, you are probably a member of Generation X.

Former President Bill Clinton and Senator Hillary Rodham Clinton are Baby Boomers. So is President George W. Bush. Senator Barack Obama is a fine example of a member of Generation X. Senator Obama has proclaimed that it is high time "his generation" were given the chance to lead the country, clearly indicating that he is not of the same generation as either the Clintons or President George W. Bush.

Love them or leave them, the Baby Boomers combined with Generation X are a very large and influential statistical group. Since the early 1970's, this massive group of individuals has flooded the nation's law schools, and ultimately, flooded the profession. The primary phenomena which drove these masses into the legal profession were a pre-conceived notion that the practice of law was the key to wealth. The Baby Boomers and Generation X got this pre-conceived notion from a well-established source: their parents. The parents of the Baby Boomers and Generation X'ers, most of whom, had returned from World War II or the Korean War, had seen enough of war and violence. Many of them having lived through the Great Depression, now wanted prosperity for themselves and for their children. They were convinced that the "professions" were the key to social and economic mobility. The professions included law and medicine, both of which they believed to be particularly lucrative. Thus, beginning at an early age, they ingrained this concept into the minds of their children. The end result: they engendered a bumper-crop of lawyers and doctors.

My own situation was no different. "Be a lawyer," my father used to say from across the dinner table, "You'll make a fortune like my cousin, Mario." I can't remember how many times I had heard this sage advice. This was almost a daily event. And my Mom would agree wholeheartedly, as she served up the pasta, which, in the 1970's, we used to call "Macaroni". She would also add her two cents saying, "I heard that cousin, Mario just put an addition on his summer home in the Hamptons." The Hamptons being a very prestigious area on the most southern tip of Long Island, N.Y. "And he bought a new boat to take from his private beach to his favorite restaurant across the bay." Cousin, Mario was also a member of the local Country Club. My father, on the other hand, had never swung a golf club, more or less sipped martinis by the side of the pool at any country club. And you can guess that the closest I had ever come to touching a golf club was a failed attempt at caddying—at; you guessed it ... Cousin Mario's Country Club.

I recall another time when cousin, Mario came home with a new Mercedes Benz. Although no one was altogether clear as to whether he bought the car or worked out some sort of a deal with someone who owed him money, my father had commented, "Probably got the car from a client." After all, clients are always indebted to their lawyers, and are always concerned, first and foremost, about paying them. Years later, I attended a Broadway production featuring a song entitled: "Pay the Lawyer". The play involved married persons fighting with each other in divorce court. The central theme song of the play was that above all things, first and foremost, the lawyer must be paid. This must be the truth, so thought I. After all, look at cousin, Mario and his mountains of cash.

I suppose it never dawned on my parents just how exactly did cousin, Mario amass all of this wealth, considering the fact that he was an attorney who never saw the inside of a courthouse. He did not work for a corporation or a large law firm. He was self-employed; had no secretary or office staff—and he hadn't received any inheritances, since everyone in our family (including cousin, Mario's parents) was middle-class at best.

How did he do it? Where did all the money come from? I do, of course, recall my parents telling me about some of cousin, Mario's "side projects", such as owning a part interest in several restaurants; owning numerous buildings in the Bronx (what you would probably describe as "slums"); owning a liquor distributorship; owning an insurance agency, and the list of his assets and businesses goes on. My parents and I always supposed that these were the "insignificant things" cousin, Mario did "on the side" when he wasn't sitting back and collecting on his lucrative law practice. After all, according to my parents, the practice of law was akin to a very good "passive investment". You earned your law degree and obtained your license, and that was pretty much the end of the real work. After that, the actual practice of law consisted of something along the lines of clipping coupons from a bond.

In the following chapters of this humble book, the fallacy of the "clipping coupons" theory will be exposed. Now this is a mandatory reading for anyone considering law as a profession.

Another aspect of the legal profession, according to my first generation Italian-American parents, was the esteem in which the general public held attorneys. "People look up to lawyers, the same as doctors", my father would stress. I have to admit he was right about one thing. People do respect lawyers about as much as they respect physicians. What I did not realize in my youth was just how badly people hate doctors.

In retrospect, I suppose that cousin, Mario was the person principally responsible ("liable", for lack of a better word) for my entering the legal profession. Even though he is, I am sure, unaware of his role in my physical, mental and emotional demise: he is nonetheless mostly to blame. But cousin, Mario is not entirely to blame. I should have learned my lesson after what should have been an enlightening incident in college. There I was, sitting in a Macro-Economics class. I don't think I can even recall the difference between "Macro" Economics and "Micro" Economics, if someone asked me today. And, I won the graduating class Award for Excellence in Economics in my college alma mater. The professor had just finished a series of lectures concerning basic economics: the standard economic fare involving capitalists, workers, and the like. The painful truth was then and there revealed to me—in retrospect, I suppose late—that the overwhelming majority of wealth in these free United States is concentrated in the hands of a miniscule segment of the population. *In short, very few persons hold very much wealth.* Most people learn this prior to high school graduation. I was always painfully slow in accepting reality. If I had a word of advice to offer a person at any stage of life, it would be to study economics. Economics is essentially the Law of Supply and Demand. *Without exception, everything in our society bases its worth upon the Law of Supply and Demand.* If one sentence could describe true wealth, it would be this: Wealth is based upon the Law of Supply and Demand. Simply put; if you have something, anything that is, which somebody else wants or desires, it is then worth something … you are worth something. You have value—and you have Wealth.

For example: you have a basketball player, like Michael Jordan, who, in his heyday, was capable of wreaking havoc upon an opposing team, and you assume that fans want their team to win, and you further assume that they are willing to pay their money to watch him play basketball, the answer is quite simple. Michael Jordan is worth a lot of money. The same holds true for seemingly useless objects. In the 1970's everybody had to have a "Pet Rock", or a "Lava Lamp". In the 1990's it was the "Tickle Me Elmo Doll" [1] that every child had to have under the Christmas Tree (now generally referred to by the members of my lawsuit-fearing profession as the religiously-neutralized "Holiday Tree"). To sum it up, it doesn't matter whether the object is actually worth anything, or how much money it takes to manufacture it or distribute it; if everybody wants it, and you are the only one who can supply it, you have the means of making a lot of money.

The same can be said of people, places and skills. For example, musicians know that Britney Spears can neither sing nor write music.[2] However, she is

---

1.   People were attacking each other in malls around the country, such as the Paramus Mall, to get these dolls of the Sesame Street character Elmo.

2.   I am a tenor, who has been trained in classical music, rock, pop and gospel. I have performed with classical choirs at Lincoln Center and Carnegie Hall in New York City, and I have performed the National Anthem at a professional baseball game.

worth plenty of money because a segment of the population either believes that she is a fine musician, or they could care less about what her "music" sounds like, so long as she wears as little clothing as possible while performing in her videos. [3]

Places can also be sources of great wealth. In fact, as you will see, places are the primary source of wealth in this country. One thing has never changed throughout the centuries: real estate creates wealth. The Queen of England and the Royal family remain wealthy today for the same reason they have been wealthy for centuries: they own a great deal of valuable real estate. Most of the "royalty" of this country also forged its wealth in real estate. [4]

To give a simple example of the value of real estate vis-à-vis "places", you can't give away large tracts of land in upstate New York. But every square inch of Manhattan real estate (which is a few hours drive away from upstate New York) is priceless. Why is every square inch of San Francisco and Marin County real estate in California priceless? As the real estate moguls tell us, it's all about the three rules of real estate value: location, location and location. It's simple really. Places such as New York and San Francisco are extremely valuable because everybody wants to live there. Places which have little value are places in which people simply do not wish to live. The concepts of "Right" or "Wrong" simply do not enter into the equation. One can create a list of pros and cons concerning just about any place, but the fact remains that if people all want very much to live in a particular place, that place is worth a lot of money. It's all about perception. And, perception is the definition of demand. [5]

In addition to places, "things" or objects can have value. A Cadillac Esplanade is worth a lot more money today than a Toyota Corolla, even though upon a simple examination, this makes little sense. The Toyota Corolla never breaks down, gets you from Point A to Point B, lasts in excess of 200,000 miles and saves you a ton of money on gasoline. A Cadillac Esplanade costs you a fortune to buy and a

---

3. The same holds true for some of the other music "Giants" of our modern area, such as Christina Aguilera, Beyonce Knowles and the like. I still, for the life of me, cannot figure out what exactly it is that "Diddy" (who used to be known as Sean Combs, then Puff Daddy, then P. Diddy) does that makes his recordings sell. This is a major recording star who can neither compose anything that vaguely resembles music, nor can he sing a note.

4. Everyone now knows that John Jacob Astor, IV was the richest man on the Titanic. But what a lot of people don't know is that his wealth was primarily derived long prior to his birth from massive New York City real estate holdings of John Jacob Astor, I. Included in this category would also be the Kennedy family, whose wealth is based to a great extent on very valuable Chicago, Illinois real estate.

fortune to drive. But, it's the car that Tony Soprano drives. It's the car Superbowl Forty MVP Hines Ward of the Pittsburgh Steelers was awarded after the big game. So everybody wants one. Again: it's all about perception, and perception equals demand.

Finally, skills can generate value, hence wealth. We have already given the example of fine skills such as those possessed by former basketball superstar Michael Jordan. But even utterly useless "skills" can generate wealth, if there is a perceived public demand. The best example I can think of is the Asian-American fellow, who, a few years ago in the first round, was kicked off the American Idol television show, a singing competition, because he could not sing a note. Yet he managed to parlay his utter lack of talent or skill, into a budding career, including recordings and celebrity appearances. In short, his "skill" was an utter lack of skill. But he made money and achieved fame nonetheless. This demonstrates, yet again, that perception and desire equal demand.[6]

Now, if we apply the Law of Supply and Demand to the practice of law, you can readily see that any one particular attorney (with the rare exception of the F. Lee Bailey, Johnny Cohran-type or John Edwards attorney) is worth very little in the marketplace *because it is a simple fact that there are just too many lawyers in this country.*[7] This means that each individual attorney's chance of success is greatly diminished as more and more lawyers enter the profession.

---

5.   Sometime in the 1970's, an enterprising young singer by the name of Peter Lemon-gello put together some recordings and started a media blitz focusing on his purported accomplishments as a singer. He stressed all of his "popular" hit records and what a well-known musician he was. The fact was that nobody had ever heard of Peter Lemongello before this brilliant media campaign. However, nobody wanted to admit that he didn't know who Peter Lemongello was. Thus, he sold many records, due to the public perception he had created. Once again, perception equals demand. And, demand translates into money for the supplier of the demand. And, perception does not have to be real. Perception simply is.

6.   I have to admit, my father got this one right. As we watched the steady decline in television during the 1980's and 1990's, my father always said if people would pay money to stare at a horse's ass on television, that is precisely what the television programmers would give us to watch. This is not far off what we are seeing on television nowadays.

7.   Recent estimates tell us that there are roughly one million lawyers in this Country. According to the most recent census figures, that translates to one lawyer for every 299 people. Japan, by contrast, has very few lawyers. And, the Japanese don't seem to be suffering as a result.

More and more lawyers continue to enter the profession because in the 1970's and 1980's, colleges and universities around the nation realized that they could capitalize on the public misperception of the "rich lawyer" so they expanded their facilities to include many new schools of law. In other words, I, along with tens of thousands of others, bought the myth and rushed in droves to these new law schools (and the old law schools, as well) to join the profession. I'll give the schools credit: they understood the Laws of Supply and Demand. However, more law schools meant, very simply, more lawyers. This dramatically increased the supply of lawyers in the marketplace (I will deal with the very important concept of "Supply" later).

Lawyers try every means at their disposal to separate themselves from the pack. Advertising is one method which burst upon the scene after the Bar Associations of many States dropped most of their restrictions on lawyer advertising. This works to a marginal degree, but it has two major drawbacks. The first problem is that it simply costs too much, and there is no guaranty of actually picking up any good cases as a result. Lawyers who advertise heavily, pay enormous advertising bills, and they spend an inordinate amount of time culling through junky cases offered to them as a result of the advertising blitz. When you give out a toll-free telephone number for people to call and you advertise a free consultation, you invite people to call. Most of the people who call either have no money to pay an attorney (so why would you want them as a client?), or they have no value to their prospective case.

Other attorneys seek to generate business by creating new areas of work which didn't previously exist. These would include the lawyers who filed the first litigations against the asbestos manufacturers; the tobacco companies; and, the brand spanking new "Fat Suits" against McDonald's Corporation and other purveyor's of so-called "Junk Food". Along these lines we now have suits against gun manufacturers, which essentially claim that a gun manufacturer is supposed to be liable each time a crook uses its gun to shoot someone. What else are guns for, if not to be shot? How is a manufacturer supposed to make a gun safe? Guns are supposed to be dangerous, aren't they? How does a manufacturer know that someone is going to fill his hunting buddy's[8] face with buck-shot (as Vice President Dick Cheney did), as opposed to taking down a flock of geese? We in the profession always wonder what could possibly be next. Will the knife manufacturers be sued next because people either cut other people or cut themselves with knives? But

---

8.   Isn't it ironic that the man Dick Cheney shot is an attorney?

aren't knives supposed to be designed to cut? Of what use would a knife be if it didn't cut?

Returning to my economics professor who in 1982 posed the question: "Who, therefore, holds the majority of wealth in our society?" I was ready with my answer. I had practiced it all my life. After all, I was going on to law school. I had been scribbling "Esquire" and "Esq." after my name since I was old enough to write. To be accepted into law school required straight A's and B+'s or so I thought. I later discovered just how wrong this concept was when I started law school. I was compelled to raise my hand and show up the rest of the class with my brilliance, and hopefully obtain an "A" in the process. As luck would have it—and the fact that the rest of the class was mostly asleep—I was called upon. I answered firmly and resolutely, "Lawyers!"

Those of you who practice law or those of you who teach economics and finance will undoubtedly find my answer astonishingly stupid and/or amusing. I vividly recall my five foot nothing professor blurting out a resounding "NO!", which nearly knocked me out of my seat. For those of you who, like my professor, know the correct answer (the correct answer is: "those who own the Means of Production"[9]), I dedicate this book. You have my admiration. You are probably wealthy, in which case you really do not need to read this book. [10] For those of you who are practicing attorneys, or unfortunate enough to be married to one (and those of you who were at one time unfortunate enough to have been married to an attorney, but are now liberated from that misery) I also dedicate this book. You have my sympathy. For those of you who are attorneys who have ceased practicing law, I dedicate this book. You have my envy. For those of you desiring to enter the profession, I also dedicate this book, and you have ... well, we will see what you have if you make it to the end of this book.

To my father's cousin, Mario: congratulations are in order for amassing substantial wealth and for convincing us suckers that you accomplished this through the practice of law. I offer my heartfelt thank you to cousin, Mario for his unwitting role in assisting my parents in their deception of me.

To my high school mathematics and computer science professor, who advised me twenty-three long years ago to "go into computers, someday soon everything will involve computers", and to my college finance and economics professor, who advised me that economics and finance would yield me a far better income than

---

9.   Those who own the Means of Production, are, quite simply, the other side of the Supply and Demand equation of wealth. They are the Suppliers.

10.   I could probably stand to read your book, however.

the practice of law; I would have done well to have listened to you. With respect to computers, back in the late 1970's few people, other than employees of NASA, had any use for computers. The closest I had ever come to a computer in the 1970's and early 1980's was playing Packman at the local bar and grill. I sincerely beg the forgiveness of Professor Robert J. Schiaffino for not heeding his sage advice. I also beg the forgiveness of my finance and economics Professor Francis J. McGrath. These people knew what they were talking about.

2

The Law School Experience: The So-Called "Socratic Method"

There is little in the real World to compare with law school. Law school is the only type of schooling where one starts at the end of a premise and works his way back to the beginning. Law professors do not "teach" law. They use the so-called "Socratic Method" as a means of transforming the "innocent" student into the belligerent, argumentative person he or she soon will be. The Socratic Method essentially has the student arguing esoteric principles of law with which the student is completely unfamiliar against a professor who has been studying these principles all of his or her adult life. The only parallel this author can draw would be that of a first year medical student being asked to perform open heart surgery on a live patient, without first examining the chest cavity of a cadaver, or better still, without ever actually having seen a representative drawing of a human heart. After all, what better way to learn than by doing? What sense is there in studying the actual anatomy of a human being first, followed by an examination of a patient who is not likely to complain or sue for malpractice, i.e., a dead person? Straight to the operating room we go. Learn while doing.

Simply put, the Socratic Method teaches absolutely nothing. It is somewhat akin to the typical psychologist's method of seeking to resolve one's problems by asking the patient: "Well, how do you feel about that?"

In my opinion, the Socratic Method should be abandoned, i.e., sent off to the scrap heap or recycling center. One thing is for certain, it should never be expanded to medical schools or to any other field involving danger to life and limb. For example, would anyone seriously consider putting the controls of a jumbo jet into the hands of a pilot who has never sat behind the seat of a plane before, not to mention never flown? Think about it. Doesn't it make sense for a prospective pilot to understand exactly why airplanes fly and how to effectuate flight before actually flying a plane? Shouldn't a pilot know why a seven hundred thousand pound piece of metal can sail through the sky at speeds of up to 600 miles per hour, at altitudes of several miles? Once we understand why airplanes fly, we can then move into the area of just exactly how we cause the airplane to fly. After we know why the airplane flies and how the airplane flies, we might try "flying" a simulated craft by computer, then work our way up to assisting other more experienced pilots, and ultimately, flying solo. Makes sense, doesn't it?

The Socratic Method would instead start out a beginning pilot with an in-depth analysis of a plane crash, and attempt to work backwards. How did the crash occur? What could we have done to have prevented the crash? How, on Earth is a person who has never piloted a plane or even studied aeronautics supposed to answer these questions? Or, those who advocate the Socratic Method would start the beginning pilot at the helm of a plane in the midst of an electrical storm, with one engine blown out and ask this novice pilot to crash land the plane. In a sense, the Socratic Method is teaching in reverse.

Another example: would society have a first year engineering student build a bridge over which thousands of people travel each day? Wouldn't it be a good idea if our engineers of tomorrow knew why bridges do what they do, and how bridges are constructed before they actually put a bridge together? Again, the Socratic Method would start the beginning engineering student with an in-depth analysis of a bridge collapse. How did the collapse occur? What could we have done to have avoided it? But, how is a beginning engineering student supposed to answer these questions when the student has no idea how bridges are built, or what materials they are constructed from, or, for that matter, why bridges stand up in the first place?

What about judges who have no training whatsoever in deciding cases, or in a particular area of the law? Read Chapter Nine.

So the Socratic Method works this way. If the subject matter is "Contracts", you do not start with what exactly a contract is. For non-lawyers, a "Contract" is an agreement between or amongst parties which must be supported by something referred to as "consideration". The agreement must be concrete, in other words, it must be a real and specific thing which is agreed to. In the example of the sale of an item of merchandise, there should be specificity as to the item to be sold, the quantity, the price and the time for performance. An example would be that of person A willing to sell a particular watch to person B for the sum of $100.00, sale to take place on December 1, 2007. The consideration for the transfer of ownership of the watch is the $100.00 sale price. We have a time for performance. We know exactly what the item to be sold is. And we know who the buyer and the seller are. Congratulations! We have a contract.

Defining the terms at issue would seem to be a meaningful starting point for any intelligent analysis. Logically, hypothetical examples of contracts should follow, until the student has a solid handle on what exactly a contract is (and what it is not), before we begin to discuss how contracts function in particular disputes involving claims of breach.[1] Finally, what occurs when people do not live up to their contracts, and what are the rights of the person who indeed did live up to his end of the bargain, would complete the course.

The Socratic Method of learning "Contracts", however, starts instead with a torturous example of how contracts do *not* work: usually the infamous <u>Garland Coal Company</u> case. This case involves the precise calculation of the monies owed by the party who did not live up to the contract to the party who did live up to the bargain. The first year student finds himself arguing in great detail about who owes how much to whom for "breach of the contract" when he or she has no idea what a contract is. The Socratic Method can be summed up by the old adage: Putting the cart before the horse. The Socratic Method teaches very little in the way of substance.[2] What it really teaches is that you need to purchase review books and read them to actually understand the course. The review books define the terms for the course and lay out the subject matter in a logical—non-Socratic—Method, so you can simply "learn" the course you signed up to take. The purveyors of these review books are yet another example of persons who have found wealth. They recognized a demand by law students desperate to learn a subject matter, which they cannot adequately learn through the age-old Socratic Method. So these entrepreneurs publish review books about every subject supposedly "taught" in law school: available at a price. You, as law students, must purchase your class books. But you'd be a fool not to also purchase the review

---

1. As Julie Andrews once sang: "Let's start at the very beginning, a very good place to start. When you read you begin with A, B, C. When you sing you begin with Do, Re, Me."

2. Conclusive proof that the Socratic Method is an utter waste of time, are the bar review courses, which are an indispensable study aid for taking the bar examination. In fact, at least in the State of New York, I cannot conceive of anyone passing the examination in the absence of having taken a bar review course, post-graduation. The mere fact that one must take one of these courses raises the question why someone cannot proceed directly to take the bar examination if one has been studying principles of law for three years full-time (four years part-time). The bar review courses, unlike the Socratic Method, teach the subject matter of the various different areas of the law in a concise and understandable manner. They set forth the various rules of law in a logical, informative fashion. In short, one can learn more from the bar review courses, in a few weeks' time, than one can learn in three years of law school.

books (incidentally, these review books are frowned upon by the professors who believe that their sage method of teaching should be all you require to master the subject). Once again, the purveyors of these review books understand the Laws of Supply and Demand and they have, as a result, found wealth. [3]

One thing the Socratic Method does teach well is how to experience humiliation. This is not necessarily a bad thing because public humiliation is something you will need to live with if you choose law as a profession.

The Socratic Method is supposed to make one "Think on one's feet", as though one could not think sitting down. This is supposed to train the law student for his or her legal career. An interesting concept, except that the overwhelming majority of time in the legal profession is spent on one's duff, as opposed to one's feet. In the wonderful World of television, the TV attorney meets with the prospective client early on in the show. The client usually has what we refer to as an "iron-clad" case, meaning that only an idiot could lose the case. About half-way through the hour long program, there is usually a "hardball" negotiation session, where the star of the show generally storms out of the conference room in a sanctimonious manner, rejecting the monetary offer made to her client as insulting. "This isn't about money" is another line we usually hear from the TV attorneys, when, in reality, *you may rest assured it is always about the money*. By the latter part of the show the case is in the midst of Trial. The attorneys are brilliant and well-spoken. The judge is sage. The typical hour long show concludes with a verdict from the jury, generally in favor of our heroes. But that doesn't matter, on those rare occasions when our heroes lose, there is more glory yet to be achieved on the inevitable appeal. And, an appeal draws better ratings.

The reality is that most civil and criminal cases take somewhat longer than one hour to conclude from the time the client hires the lawyer. Most civil cases take from 1 year, on the extremely low side, to upwards of 4 to 5 years or more to conclude. Some cases take even longer than that. Perhaps the record for stagnation of cases can be found in our friendly State of New York, where only recently, the

---

3.   It has been observed that if law school professors actually taught the subject matter of their courses to the students, instead of trying to twist and contort it out of them via the Socratic Method, the period of time from commencing one's studies to graduation could be cut by at least one half. This, of course, would never happen, because an entire economy depends upon not only the staggering number of law students entering our law schools nowadays but also upon their spending three to four years at those schools. Heavily dependent upon that economy are law school professors, who would never take any action that could possibly reduce their tenure, or worse, possibly result in their actually having to enter the work-force and practice law.

last civil cases were disposed of from the Attica State prison riots of the 1970's. These cases were heard in what New York State refers to as the "Court of Claims". The Court of Claims is the only court wherein a private litigant may sue the State of New York for most civil claims. It is also a great money-saving device for the State of New York since it takes so long for these cases to be resolved. Since the State gets to hang onto the money during the substantial period of delay, without the payment of interest in the situation of a personal injury case, this is a huge cost-saving device.

Clients are generally in the dark as to what transpires between hiring of the attorney and the eventual trial date. This is not surprising. Many, many years ago, a summons meant just that: the defendant (the person being sued) was literally dragged into court by a Marshal or other court officer and set down for a trial, at which he had to explain why he should not be made to pay money to the claiming party (called the "Plaintiff"). Most jurists thought that this was a bit harsh, and rightfully so. Over the years, our system of civil justice has evolved (some would say "devolved") into a situation where there is far too much time between the filing of a case and the actual trial, when the case is finally heard and concluded. The end result is that justice is a very slow and cumbersome process where the attorneys spend months and years shuffling papers and making meaningless court appearances before a case is ever called to trial.

Returning to the Socratic Method of teaching for a moment. I always found that the Socratic Method of teaching had but one beneficiary: the professor. It is infinitely easier to torture a pack of intimidated students with hypothetical questions than to actually teach the subject matter of the course. In this respect, law school is somewhat akin to the Marine Corps Boot Camp. One is tortured for the sole purpose of testing one's so-called "character" and resolve. From day one students end up dividing themselves into essentially two groups. The first group are the people who love to hear the sound of their own voices and who believe that they possess the wisdom of the ages. Law school exists as a forum for their wise opinions. The second group is the Claude Rains group. These are the students, like me, who tried to stay out of the professor's line of sight during lectures. We tried to be invisible. It rarely worked. My friends in the Marine Corps tell me it doesn't work there either.

Paranoia

Law schools are fueled by the frenetic energy of paranoia. There are few creatures in this World more paranoid than the first year law student. The first year student believes everything negative that is told to him or her, and lives in dire fear of the dark unknown. Gossip laced with horror stories abound. These stories are generally untrue and their source is usually the upper-class students, who enjoy themselves at the expense of the first year students: much the same way these persons were abused by upper-class students when they themselves were first year students. And, so the vicious cycle continues[4]. First year students will believe just about anything they hear since they are so terrified of the unknown. They believe that the professors sit up all night conceiving tortures and punishments for miscreant students. In reality, the professors generally come in several sizes, shapes and colors: (1) those who are unable to practice law in the so-called "business" or "real" World; (2) those who are unwilling to practice law; (3) those who are practicing law but need a little extra money; (4) those who were law clerks to federal judges and live for the endless debate of esoteric principles of law; (5) those whose families have thrived on trust accounts for decades and who need something to do with their time when they aren't playing golf or sailing; and, (6) those who live for the endless pursuit of younger students of the opposite sex. This last group has traditionally consisted of balding, paunchy middle-aged to older male professors.

As with paranoia in general, there is no real basis for the law school paranoia. Nor is there any basis to fear the professors. Nor is there any basis for the continued use of the ridiculous so-called Socratic Method. In my opinion, if wise old Socrates were to sit through a modern law school class, he would be horrified. It is time to finally recognize that Socrates is dead and that we should administer the poison hemlock to the Socratic Method as well.

Cut Throat Students

Not part of the curriculum, but the lesson is learned the first week of law school. I liken it to the person who burns the bridge behind him so that nobody else can cross over. One of the first assignments in law school is to rummage through the law library to find a particular case or statute. You had better get there first. If you don't, you'll either find a blank space between book number 453 and 455 (your assignment was to find book 454, page 301) or you may find book 454, but page 301 will be missing: removed from the book, i.e., torn out. The rationale of the student who purloined the page (or the entire book) is not so much to prove that

---

4.   Could this be training for our future "vicious" lawyers?

he or she got the assignment correct. *Rather, it is to insure that he or she is the ONLY student who got the assignment correct.*

This lovely tradition of sabotaging others in their efforts at achieving success, carries through to the profession. If you have ever visited a courthouse law library, you will notice that a fair portion of the books are located behind the librarians' desk. These are usually the more popular books: the books most likely to be needed for research in that particular jurisdiction. For example, if you are in New York, the "hidden" books are usually the New York statutes, as opposed to the Alaskan statutes, which no one could care less about, even if you live in Alaska, I suppose. [5]

These books are hidden because the attorneys have a tendency to steal them, if they are left in with the general population of books. For those of you who believe I am jumping to conclusions, one only needs to look at the books which are generally missing from any particular law library. If one practices in the New York State court system, for example, books and publications customarily missing from a New York law library would include what is known as the Civil Practice Law and Rules (the "Bible" of civil practitioners); the New York Law Journal (a daily periodical and a must for practicing attorneys); and, Martindale-Hubbell (a publication which lists lawyers and gives biographical and rating information about them). Since lawyers need these books so desperately, and they are so expensive to maintain in one's own library, the demand for these items is high. This, coupled with the fact that these books are virtually always missing from the library, leads one to the inevitable conclusion that the attorneys have "removed" the books. After all, what would your average electrician do with the Civil Practice Law and Rules? For that matter, why would your average electrician even be in a courthouse library to begin with? In summary, the lesson in throat-cutting one learns in law school is well-reserved for future use.

The Professors

Law school professors seem to have the market cornered on the bizarre. They are the legal geeks. These are people you would never invite to a social function. The general rule of thumb is that the more homely the professor the more lecherous he is likely to be. Having been raised in a rather sheltered household, I was always surprised to see some of the more attractive female members of my law school

---

5.   Personally, I don't even know if there is any law in the State of Alaska, and if there is, who would enforce it? And, against whom would it be enforced: Orcas?

class engaged in after-hours "workshops" and "study projects" with one or more of these repugnant nebbishes. I never quite understood the coincidence between the unusually high grades these students received from a particular professor (and how they always managed to be in that particular professor's class year after year) while the remainder of their grades were sorely lacking.

There are rather few attractive professors teaching in our law schools today. This is consistent with the profession as a whole. There are few, if any, Dylan McDermotts ("The Practice"), Calista Flockharts ("Ally McBeal"), Robert Redfords ("Legal Eagles") or James Spaders ("Boston Legal") in the profession and certainly none in the law schools. The only attractive female professor I can recall from law school was our Dean. The Dean, a former judge, somehow managed to maintain a virtually flawless figure well into her fifties. She also had a penchant for wearing revealing bright red outfits, resulting in her being dubbed "The Scarlet Harlot"—all behind her back, of course. Lest the reader conclude that the Dean's nickname was an offensive sexist remark conjured up by the male students, I recall several of the female students having come up with the nickname.

The Study Groups

Law students are constantly seeking magic formulas and elixirs that will convert as little study time as possible into winning grades. Unfortunately, the truth is that there are no such magic formulas and those who spend much of their time seeking them usually end up with sub-par grades. In short, you cannot have both any semblance of a "life" and also obtain good grades in law school.

It doesn't take long for the so-called "Study Groups" to emerge. In theory, a study group is supposed to be a group of students who congregate for the purpose of bettering their studies, under the old adage: "Two heads are better than one". Unfortunately, in practice, these groups rarely work. A fly on the wall of an after-hours study group would observe the following. The study group starts with several members voicing their opinion on what they believe will be tested at the end of the semester exam. The natural leader of the group (the Alpha Male or Female) will reveal that he or she has been in contact with former students and upper-class students and that he or she has studied the exams given in previous years by the same professor. The leader will boldly proclaim precisely what will appear on the final exam. The rest of the group will agree and that will be the end of the "study" portion of the study group. The group members will congratulate themselves on being so witty and so very prepared for the exam. They will laughingly lament the unfortunate individuals who are not part of their study group. The remainder of the time spent in the study group will be little more than a reenactment of teen-age mating rituals.

Students dating other students in law school is rampant. This is like looking for love in all the wrong places. Yet it is a natural result of being cooped up day after day and night after night with the same people. Law school also has a tendency to make and break marriages. I recall at least half a dozen couples who met in law school and then subsequently married. I recall at least an equal number of married persons who, as a result of law school, became divorced persons.

3

The Bar Examination: You mean the Whole Thing comes down to a few hours?

Yes, it's true. The three years you have suffered through in law school (four if you were crazy enough to have worked a full-time job and simultaneously attended night classes), does indeed come down to a two day test known as the bar examination (three days, if you are taking the California bar exam). Of course, everyone knows that you can take the examination several times until you pass it. However, failing the bar examination the first time only adds to the expected paranoia that you had when you first sat for the exam. Thus, with each successive failed attempt, your emotional well-being goes further and further downhill, resulting in less and less of a chance of passage each time. In short, this is a test you do not want to have to take more than once. The other reason you want to pass the test on the first attempt is that the law firm you have joined has undoubtedly set a maximum number of attempts for its associates before the new hire is terminated. The firm has hired you because it wants to have you do the work of an attorney. The firm wants to bill its clients an attorney's hourly rate for your work. The firm has not hired you as a paralegal. The longer it takes for you to pass the bar examination, the less profitable the situation is for the firm.

As you can imagine, those who take the bar examination wait with little patience for the results. They want to pass. They want to be winners. If you joined a large law firm (which hires fifteen to thirty first year associates each August) you don't want to be the only first year associate at the firm who didn't pass.

Rest assured, if you didn't pass the exam, everyone at the firm will somehow find out. They will scan the posted list of those persons who passed the exam until they find, or don't find, your name. Then, the word will spread throughout the firm like an Arizona wild-fire.

In reality, the real winners in connection with the bar examination are not the students who pass the test, but rather the entire cottage industry which has grown up around the exam. This industry markets what are called "Bar Review Courses", and there are as many different companies selling these courses as there are types of courses to take. You can take one course that teaches you how to take the bar exam. You can take another course that teaches you what is going to be on the bar exam. You can take a course that teaches you how to answer essay questions.[1] You can take a course on how to write—which you would assume most law students would know after three years of graduate school. You would be surprised. You can take a course on how to answer multiple choice questions. You can take courses on how to stay focused and relaxed for the exam. There are even books about the various bar review courses themselves! You can take all of the foregoing choices. In fact, you are highly encouraged to by the organizations marketing these courses. Given the level of paranoia rampant in the profession, and in those who have completed law school, the marketing of these courses is not difficult. "Are you sure you have taken the right course?" "Don't let yourself be failed on the basis of one essay." "Don't let the multiple choice questions prevent you from passing the bar exam." "Are you certain you can survive without our course?" "Are you sure you have studied enough for the exam?" Such marketing slogans abound. The old Clint Eastwood film comes to mind wherein Eastwood points his gun at the bad guy and asks him how many bullets he thinks have been fired and if he believes that there are any bullets remaining in the clip. Eastwood then poses the question: "You have to ask yourself, do I feel lucky?"

It is amazing the number of students who are convinced that they will be the one out of ten thousand persons who fails the bar examination by one (1) point. No one seems to spend too much time worrying about whether he will get the entire exam or most of it wrong. The bar exam courses play into this frenzy: "Maybe our course can be the difference in your passing, or failing!" "What if it all came down to one point?"

In retrospect, had I known how profitable these bar review courses were, I would have skipped law school altogether and set up my own course instead. Naturally, most students sign up for whatever courses they can. The strangest phenomena is that the persons who sign up for the greatest number of courses usually end up failing by one or two points because they spend so much time

---

1.   I always liked this one. If you have no idea how to answer an essay question, how did you make it through college to begin with? How were you accepted to law school? How did you make it through law school?

running around from course to course location, they have little time left to actually spend studying anything. I remember a very bright student by the name of Sam (we will stick with his first name only) who was without a doubt the single most paranoid person I have ever met. Sam was one of those people who couldn't say he was graduated in the top ten percent of the class because he was somewhere in the eleventh percentage. Sam couldn't say he was a member of the honor society[2] since only 34 persons were selected, and, you guessed it, Sam ended up number 35. He signed up for every bar review course available. He spent a fortune on these courses. He spent all his time running from place to place as opposed to actually sitting down and learning the material. The end-result: he failed the bar examination by one (1) point. This was exactly what I expected.

A word to the wise: if you find yourself in the position of someone who has graduated from law school and is about to take the bar exam: take one good course and study, study, study. If you do that, and you weren't a complete screw up in school, you should pass the test. Even if you didn't get anything whatsoever out of the Socratic Method, and, as I have stated previously, I don't know how anyone in his right mind could, you still have time to learn just what you need to know from the bar review course, in order to pass the exam. Take one good course, and study, study, study. Remember: Paranoia will destroy Ya.

---

2. In law school, they refer to the honor society as the "Law Review". Everyone wants to "make" law review. However, the law review results in adding to the student's burden to get work done because in addition to your regularly-assigned class-work, you are mandated to author an article or treatise on some obscure aspect of the law. This can take weeks of valuable time out of the law review member's schedule. Law students, in general, have very little social life. Law review members have no social life whatsoever.

4

Entering the Profession

The Large Law Firm: Getting one's feet wet (and one's social life dry)

Three years of law school have gone by, the bar examination (or examinations, if you took the examinations of more than one State) is over, and you're still alive. By this time, you have lost most, if not all, of the friends you started school with. In their stead you now have "colleagues". Colleagues are essentially persons similarly situated to oneself who could really care less if you live or die, so long as they are not held liable. They too have lost most, if not all, of their friends along the way, so this is your common ground. You are equally miserable, and this is supposed to be a good starting point for your new relationships.

If you were married at the time you started law school, the odds are very good that you are not now. If you are still married after law school, it is most likely that you are married to a different person than when you started. At a minimum, you are not married to the same person. Law school has a tendency to break up marital relationships, and replace them with flimsy coalitions, driven more by immediate need and expediency than anything of substance. Most likely your relatives have gone down the same path as your friends. You have become a pariah.

Most people with any sense of self-respect do not want to have anything to do with you. No one wants you around. As bad as this seems, there is a ray of hope. Law school has done you a great service by training you for the manner in which people will treat you for the rest of your life, or at least for the duration of your professional life—which as you will see herein is really the same thing. It is also good training for the typical starting point in any legal career: you enter the "Large Law Firm".

Just a side note on the friends you have left behind three (or four) years ago. They have been making money all this time at their respective careers or paths of life, setting up networks, socializing and in many instances marrying and doing the things living people do. Your life, on the other hand, has been on hold. And, unless you had wealthy parents or a "sugar-daddy" bankrolling your law school tuition, you are under mountains of debt. You feel compelled to enter a profession where you can at least start to pay back this burdensome debt you now find yourself swimming in. You feel compelled to enter the legal profession, even if you hated law school but stuck it out as a matter of pride, or because your parents wouldn't hear of your quitting, or for whatever reason. You believe that the law will help you pay off this debt and ultimately become wealthy. You still have not figured out that mastering the Laws of Supply and Demand is the true basis of wealth. Remember: the larger the demand and the scarcer the supply makes for a more valuable product or service. You and your newfound colleagues now flood the legal profession, thereby expanding the supply, in essence, making the prospects of your own individual wealth less likely.

The simple fact is that there are too many lawyers in the marketplace. The Laws of Supply and Demand dictate that the chance of any individual lawyer achieving wealth is slim.

But, where are all these lawyers, you ask? Well, a quick glance at the sheer number of "Large Law Firms" (usually defined as a group of lawyers in excess of 100 at any given location) will show you just how concentrated the legal field is. To this massive figure must be added all the lawyers from "mid-sized firms" (usually defined as between 25 and 50 lawyers); plus small firm lawyers (2-25 lawyers); the staggering number of sole practitioners; plus government lawyers (such as District Attorneys, United States Attorneys; State, County and Town/City Attorneys) and the so-called "non-practicing" lawyers. This does not answer the question of *why* we have so many lawyers in this country, you may be thinking. I am still asking myself that same question.

Many lawyers start out at the large law firms for essentially two reasons: 1. The rational reason: the large law firms hire a lot more people than the smaller firms, and this was the only place you could get a job. These firms also pay higher starting salaries; or, 2. The irrational reason: you have an innate love of the large firm predatory environment and you want to spend the rest of your days tormenting those beneath you, while being devoured by those above you.

Your law school "Placement Office", as they usually call the people who are supposed to help you get a job after law school, has not necessarily looked out for your best interest in setting up your interviews. You see, the placement office gets more credit if it "places you" with a large law firm than it does if it places you with a small law firm. Placement offices and law schools keep statistics as to the types of firms which hire their respective graduates. Placing a larger percentage of the student body with the large law firms is something of a status symbol. It is something the law school used in their marketing efforts to convince you to attend their school as opposed to some other law school, which supposedly didn't place its students as well. Therefore, you can rest assured that your school's placement office will do all it can to convince you to interview with the large law firms, and to take a position with one of them should it be offered to you. Another reason placement offices want you to work for the large law firms is that if you sweat it out and stay with these firms you may be of assistance with future placements of students from your alma mater. You also have a better shot at becoming a financial contributor to your law school.

What *not* to expect when you start: The evening before I started with a large, New York City law firm, I decided to attend the movies. The year was 1986 and the hot movie playing that Summer, was "Legal Eagles", starring Robert Redford, Debra Winger and Darryl Hannah. For anyone who has seen the film, I can say without equivocation that the reality of the practice of law is diametrically opposed to what is portrayed in the movie. After twenty-one years of practice, I have yet to have an affair with any client who looked anything like Darryl Hannah. Nor have I set up partnership with anyone who looked anything like Debra Winger. One aspect of the film, however, has indeed come to fruition, that is, the insomnia. The film has wonderful scenes depicting the epic battles waged by the characters portrayed by Debra Winger and Robert Redford, as they each seek to clear their racing minds of the day's events and get a restful night's sleep. Robert Redford's character tap-dances on the bathroom floor to get to sleep. Debra Winger's character drinks wine in front of the TV set all night. The legal profession is indeed a fertile breeding ground for insomnia. Or, if you prefer to view the cup as half full, you might look at it as the cure for narcolepsy.

Day One: The Orientation. This isn't what they taught me in Law School!

Your final summer in the human race is over, and you now enter the large law firm's "Orientation Program". Those of you who didn't spend the entire summer after law school on the beach but instead worked in the legal profession now realize that this was a terrible mistake. After all, you were given an offer of employment during your final year of school. You didn't actually have to do anything after that point, except take (and hopefully pass) the bar examination. If you seized the opportunity to travel or simply lie on the beach doing nothing or chase members of the opposite sex (or members of the same sex, depending upon your sexual orientation), you at least started out your legal career well-rested. You are in better shape, from an emotional standpoint, than those who spent the last vacation of their lives outside the law actually working at a law firm. This latter group is now starting to question whether they really want to do this for a living, and couldn't they find a career which would pay a decent wage, and yet keep them closer to the beach?

"Orientation" is the insidious process by which the large law firm attempts to turn each one of you into one of them. I say "one" of them, because individuality is very much frowned upon at the large firms. The firm itself has a "Collective Personality" and you had better learn exactly what that personality is, and quickly, if you seek to survive. Once you determine what the collective personality is, you must make it your own, or you will have no chance of becoming a "Partner" someday: the supposed goal of all newcomers to the law firm.

The First Assignment: Briefcase Carriers; Note-Takers; Proofreaders and Researchers

Your first assignment with the large law firm can be relatively mundane, such as carrying the briefcase of a more senior associate, who in turn is carrying the brief-case of a junior partner, who in turn is carrying the briefcase of a more senior partner to court. The senior partner is ostensibly "handling the case", but what this really means is that if the case is successful, the kudos go entirely to the senior partner. If the case is unsuccessful, the blame trickles down to the junior partner, to the senior associate, and—you guessed it—to you. Thus, being a senior partner is a great thing from any standpoint. There is no comparison between the pay you are receiving as a junior associate and the compensation package of a senior partner. Senior partners are collecting (some would argue "earning") at least ten to twenty times what you are being paid. Senior partners can actually take vacations. You, as a junior associate, are usually allotted somewhat less vacation time, and then told by the firm: "We encourage you to take your vacation time". However, if you actually use the vacation time, the law firm keeps a record of this against you for future use. It becomes generally understood that, even though the law firm officially encourages you to take vacation time, the firm really does not want you to take any time off. It is sort of like being the last person in a restaurant at closing time where the waiter asks if you would like more coffee. You do want the coffee but you are expected to say no.

Senior partners also enjoy other perks that junior associates (and even junior partners, for that matter) are forbidden. For one thing, senior partners are allowed to guffaw as loudly as they want at law firm "Holiday" parties (the term "Christmas Party" seems to have been phased out starting in the mid-1990's). Although great inroads have been made against sexual harassment of employees in recent years, you are still, as a senior partner, permitted some leeway in so far as acting in a lewd manner toward younger members of the opposite sex. Of course, you as the senior partner would be the first person to fire an associate who behaved in the same manner as yourself. The real check on the behavior of senior partners is how much money they are bringing into the law firm coffers. As long as a senior partner commands a client base that churns out the expected revenue, the partner is invincible. But should that partner's accounts dry up, he or she becomes as expendable as anyone else. Several years ago Judd Nelson starred in a film[1] as an attorney who was being considered for partnership at a large, prestigious law firm. In a behind closed doors meeting, all of the partners—except one—agreed that Nelson's character was unorthodox, unconventional and downright weird and that they did not wish him to be elevated to the ranks of partner. The lone dissenting partner then asked the firm's accountant to stand up. The accountant spoke briefly about the substantial revenues being generated by the proposed new partner. The scene closes with Judd Nelson's character celebrating his elevation to the partnership. *Rest assured, senior partners are all about money.*

When you join the large law firm you have to understand that you have given up most, if not all, of your autonomy. Large law firms are not democracies. No one is really interested in your point of view or your suggestions. The decisions are all made by a committee, sometimes known as an "Executive Committee", which is somewhat akin to the corporate counterpart of the same name or a Board of Directors. Even the executive committee can be somewhat of a misnomer since the real power in a large firm, as you will find out, is generally in the hands of a very small group of persons: sometimes *one person*.

The fun thing about the large firm experience is that no one tells you any of these things when you start. No one will tell you who is really in charge of things, what not to say to this particular person, and what to say to that one. No one will tell you how to act, or dress, or speak, or not to speak. No one will tell you about the real nature of "vacation" time. You are supposed to pick these things up by the process of osmosis. You are also supposed to learn the appropriate "Firm Behavior" from more senior associates at the firm. This is, of course, ridiculous, because these persons are in direct competition with you to make partner at the firm. They want you to screw up and look like an ass to the higher-ups. If you

---

1.   The film was "From the Hip", 1987.

don't make partner, they have a better chance of doing so. Dumping junior associates in with more senior associates is like dropping the chicken into the fox's den.

Let's return to the initial assignments. Carrying briefcases can be a rewarding exercise. While most associates feel this is degrading, it is one of the rare opportunities for you, as a junior associate, to temporarily have a higher earning capacity than any other type of worker performing a similar task. Think about it. A beginning construction worker has to carry lumber and tools and the like for the more senior union workers in the trade, but he doesn't have a starting salary between $75,000.00 and $175,000.00 to do it. So, if you find yourself carrying briefcases, or sitting at a trial taking notes and trying to look astute, while someone else tries the case (the note-taking usually goes along with carrying the briefcase), my advice to you is to sit back and enjoy the experience. If you could spend twenty years carrying briefcases (with salary increases and cost of living increases) you might be earning an average of between $200,000.00 to $300,000.00 per annum and never have to actually handle a case. If your money is properly invested—you haven't blown it all trying to entertain yourself during the miserable years of being an associate—you may be able to retire. Not bad.

Next, there are the associates who have the ball and chain affixed to their extremities from day one. They are chained to a cubicle in the firm's law library. Their job, for so long as they should remain at the firm, or for so long as they remain alive, is to do research projects for the more senior attorneys. This breed of cat may also be an over-qualified proof-reader. One may spend years checking for typographical errors in Securities and Exchange Commission (SEC) filings, for example. This type of associate tends to gain weight immediately, because he or she is not permitted to move more than a matter of a few feet from the workstation. Also, the work is so boring that the mere pleasure of eating brightens an otherwise droll day. Depression runs rampant in these ball and chain associates. The tendency to quit also is highest in these associates. The firm knows this and could really care less. The firm knows you will probably quit, but your cubicle can be filled easily from next year's law school crop and at a lower price. No problems there.

The Sneak Attack Victims

Another type of associate is the rare breed which has been designated for the baptism by fire. This is rarely ever the fate of attractive young female associates who are usually assigned to work for paunchy, middle-aged male partners. The reason is obvious. The partner doesn't want to send this associate out of the firm on errands. He wants to keep her around where he can see her.[2] The sneak attack victim associate arrives at work one morning to find a portion of a file sitting on his desk with a short note to the effect that the case is on some court's calendar that morning (usually in about 30 minutes). There is usually a very brief, and not at all helpful, description of what it is that the associate is supposed to do when he or she arrives at court. There is also a direction to the associate to "handle the matter". The person who "planted" the file on the junior associate's desk is rarely, if ever, around to explain in more detail. The portions of the file needed to properly handle the situation are usually missing. This is an example of the old dump and run play.

The junior associate takes off for his first court appearance. He attempts to quickly scan the file on the subway train or while driving in his car on the way to court. He gathers that some party to the lawsuit has asked the court for some relief, and his firm does not wish to agree to this request. He has been instructed to "adjourn" the court date. Of course, no one bothers to mention to him that lawyers cannot simply "adjourn" court appearances: only courts can do this. The lawyers can agree to an adjournment, in which case the court will most likely, but not always, go along with the postponement. The junior associate sees a note in the file where his adversary (this is the attorney for the other side) will agree to the request for the postponement. He breathes a sigh of relief. He has found the court, and made his way to the correct courtroom. This may not sound like much, but in a large city there are usually several locations for the same court. To make matters worse, you usually do not know what courtroom, or for that matter, what courthouse your particular judge will be in until the morning of the court appearance. This is so because the courthouse personnel are constantly changing the courtroom assignments for the judges. I have always been of the opinion that they do this to get some humor into their otherwise dull lives: they get to watch the attorneys scramble around trying to find the right courtroom, and they get to enjoy the judge's chastising of the attorneys who are late, even though the courtroom was changed that very morning, or the elevators were not working, or the like. It's good sport.

But in any event, our junior associate has managed to make it on time to the correct courtroom: so far so good. Now, it begins to settle in that this is his very first court appearance. The panic really begins to set in when he remembers that

---

2.   Women have undoubtedly made significant inroads in the law. However, the overwhelming majority of the senior partners at the large law firms today are still men.

although he has passed the bar examination, he hasn't actually been "sworn in" yet. The swearing in ceremony occurs at the courthouse at which the new attorney is administered the oath. It is only after taking the oath that one actually becomes an attorney. If you had any doubt about the staggering number of attorneys entering the profession, any such doubt should be removed at the swearing-in ceremony, where hundreds of lawyers are packed into a large courtroom to take the oath. Remember the Laws of Supply and Demand? So, technically, our "attorney" appearing in the above-example, is not really an attorney. Yet, he has been asked to do an attorney's job. In short, he is practicing law without a license. This is a crime in most states.

He is convinced that the judge must know he is not an attorney. It's written all over his face. Besides, judges know everything, right? What does he say if the judge asks him: "Are you, in fact, admitted to practice in this jurisdiction?" Does he stand up before the Judge and say: "Your honor, I am the *attorney* representing the defendant in this matter." No good. "Your honor, I am representing the defendant in this matter." Just as bad. "Your honor, I am here for the defendant in this matter." This is passable. We will have to go with this one. In any event, since we are only going to adjourn the motion anyway, it should not make a difference. I will be in and out of the court quickly and painlessly, he thinks.

The only problem is that his adversary has neglected to show up to court. One way or the other, the adversary is not there. This happens more often than one would think. Now, when his case is called, instead of his adversary telling the judge what the case is about, and making it so that all he has to do is say "I agree" or "I consent", our young associate is going to have to carry the ball. His case is called, and he tells the judge that he wants the matter adjourned. The judge tells him it does not make any sense to adjourn the motion since his adversary is not present. Therefore, he should "proceed". The judge peers forward with an incredulous look on his face when he hears that the attorney does not wish to proceed in default of his adversary. Finally, and reluctantly, the judge tells the young attorney to make sure that someone who is familiar with the file comes back to court on the adjourned date. Thank God that's over! The first court appearance is down. Not exactly what you see in the movies. Little does the junior associate know, but this is just the beginning of his adventures with the firm. *In fact, he will never handle a case from start to finish.* That wouldn't make sense because he might actually become familiar with the case, and he wouldn't be in a position to be ambushed. From here on in he will spend the early years of his career picking up last-minute court appearances from other attorneys on cases he knows nothing about. The firm believes that this sort of thing is good for young associates. It forces them to "think on their feet".

The Night Shift

Many persons voluntarily work the night-shift at newspaper offices, hospitals, all-night gasoline service stations, and the like. These persons come in two varieties: those who are the least senior in their organization; and, those who love the reverse style of life. But these persons all have one thing in common: if they work the night-shift, they are allowed to sleep during the day. Unfortunately, this is not the case with the large law firm night-shift. There will be no sweet sounds coming down on this nightshift. When a junior associate works the night-shift, this means that he or she has most likely worked the day shift the prior workday, and will work the day shift the next day as well. Night shift means round-the-clock work. This 24/7 work is usually reserved for the male associates and unattractive female associates, unless a particular partner is attempting to arrange a night-time tryst with one of the more attractive associates.

Working the round-the-clock work-shift is sort of like the emperor's new clothes. The associates who performed these feats of endurance must act the day after as though they are perfectly well and not in the least tired. The partners who engaged these night-hawks on their vigil will treat them as though they had just returned from a Caribbean vacation. These night-hawks are easy to spot since they usually have no make-up, or haven't shaved; they have the standard dark circles under the eyes, and their clothes looked slept in. Everyone pretends not to notice that the emperor is naked. The worst part about working the night-shift at the large law firm is that if you do it once, each one of the higher-ups will assume you will do it again for him or her. Thus, instead of spreading the "wealth" of night assignments around, the senior partners tend to assign these projects again and again to the same persons. The end result is that you become a robotic partner some eight to ten years down the line (assuming you have survived); or, you become another statistic in the firm's attrition records (i.e., you quit); or, you suffer a mental breakdown.

Policy

Large law firms thrive on the basis of "Policy". The best working definition of policy I can give is this: "Policy" is little more than a convenient way for your employer to tell you that no matter how much practical sense your proposal or suggestion makes, it is simply not going to be implemented. Policy stands as a wall against making improvements to an organization which are simply too much work or too much effort to implement. The general rule is this: if your suggestion or proposal is going to cause some do-nothing bureaucrat any extra effort whatsoever, even if it's worthwhile, it isn't going to happen.

Large law firms abound in policies. Each policy is usually an overreaction to something that happened in the past. For example, a lot of firms nowadays have a "No Dating" policy. This probably came about because everyone is so paranoid about being sued for sexual harassment; it is a lot easier to simply tell people they cannot date. What the policy doesn't take into account is the fact that associates starting out at the firm are usually in their early twenties. These folk are mostly single, and since they spend every waking moment of their lives at the firm, they could not possibly be expected to interact with any form of human life outside the firm. Moreover, they certainly didn't make (or keep) any lasting relationships during law school. What's more, the firm tries to capitalize on supposedly non-working time of these junior associates as well. On the rare occasions when junior associates are not working, they are attending seminars and other droll client functions. So we have the typical scenario where two young, single associates, who spend approximately eighty hours each week at the firm, get to know and like each other. They want to date. Now, one of these persons has to leave the firm in order for them to date, or they have to sneak around and hope not to be caught by the powers that be. This is a far cry from the married seventy year old male partner trying to coerce the twenty-four year old female associate into having sex with him as a condition to advancement within the firm. The latter being a rational basis for the "No Dating" policy.

But the no dating policies generally backfire because the first pair discussed above, the young, single associates, usually have the policy enforced against them, as though they were doing something morally or ethically wrong. But, as you guessed, the policy isn't likely to be enforced against the lecherous senior partner: that is unless he stops bringing in money to the firm.[3]

Most policies are preposterous. One day the large firm in which I first worked after law school, sent a written policy around to all persons at the firm. Every voucher for reimbursement of expenses had to be signed by a senior partner, or the voucher was invalid. Eager to point out the insanity of this new "Policy", I

---

3.   You will see that senior partners are generally "exempt" from most rules and policies at the firm, that is, unless they stop bringing in the dough, so to speak. When even the most senior partners stop bringing in money to the firm, they become *persona non grata*. They can then be treated as though they were junior associates.

approached a very senior partner with an expense voucher seeking a refund to me of $2.00 I had laid out on the firm's behalf to park my car at one of the court-houses I was sent to. I was promptly thrown out of the partner's office—after he signed the voucher. I never heard anything further on that policy.

This firm also had a peculiar policy of requiring every person to tap into his or her telephone the full case code on each case for which a telephone call was being made.[4] This number would be followed by the attorney's assigned "number" with the firm. While this may not seem such a big deal at first glance, the case codes were about ten digits in length, and the attorney code was four digits in length (it was three when I started, then increased to four due to the sheer magnitude of the associate mass). This meant that for a telephone call outside one's area code, the attorney had to dial 25 numbers in the exactly correct order to get the call through. All day long, one would hear the cursing of attorneys who would get to maybe the sixteenth number before a mistake was made, and then he would have to dial the entire number sequence all over again. And, God forbid one dialed the wrong number. You also had to key in these numbers just to make a photocopy. God forbid the firm might have to suck up a nickel to make a photocopy when the client is being billed thousands of dollars in legal fees. I always waited for the day when associates would have to use a client code in order to obtain toilet paper in the firm bathrooms. I left the firm in 1988, so it is entirely possible that this policy has since been instituted.

The Magic of Client Billings

This is what large law firms do best. Large law firms have enormous overhead. Most of the overhead is in the form of compensation packages for the senior partners. Following the expense of the senior partners is usually the rent on the firm's office spaces (usually multiple offices). Rest assured the bill to run the office is staggering. Someone has to pay for it. You guessed who. The clients have to pay the bill, but it is the responsibility of the individual attorneys in the firm to make sure that happens. Thus, the pressure on associates at the large law firms to create billable hours is huge.

---

4.   A word about numbers: Everything at large law firms revolves around numbers. A client is assigned a client number. Each attorney is assigned an attorney number. Each separate case is assigned a case number. No one at the firm seems to be able to locate any information about a case or client in the absence of the appropriate number.

Think of it as a triangle. At the peak of the triangle is the most senior partner or partners. At the base of the triangle are the masses of junior associates. As you guessed, the work flows down the triangle and the overwhelming bulk of the money flows up the triangle.

Firms live by the "billable hour". So what then is a "billable hour"? A "billable hour" is not supposed to be the same thing as an ordinary hour on this Earth. There are twenty-four hours in a day, but, of course, no one could actually work on a file, or combination of files, for twenty-four hours in one work day, could he? Well, the answer is No, and Yes.

You see, attorney billable hours are usually divided into segments, called "minimum increments". It works this way: if an attorney spends one minute reading a letter which has been received by him on your case, he bills you either six minutes (what is referred to as .10 billing—or tenths billing), or he bills you fifteen minutes (what is referred to as .25 billing—or quarters billing). Not bad. Therefore, in the example of a .25 billing minimum, if it takes your attorney one minute to read the letter, he has billed you for fifteen minutes of his time. There-fore, in one minute of Earth time, your attorney has billed fifteen minutes, or 15 times the actual amount of time it took to accomplish the task. Travel and in-court appearances make this even more interesting. If one travels from New York to Tokyo on a particular case, one bills the entire trip to the client. The client is, of course, billed at the attorney's hourly rate for the plane flight. And, the client has to pay for the plane fare as well. Let's say the plane flight is twenty-two hours in length. Let's also say that your attorney has brought work for other clients with him and that he does this other work for ten of the twenty-two hours in flight. Thus, at the end of the twenty-two hours, your attorney has billed a minimum of thirty-two hours: twenty-two to the Tokyo client, and ten to someone else. Are you interested yet? I could never calculate this well, but as a result of various time zone differences one can bill even more time depending upon the point of origin and the point of destination. Court time has a similar result. If I go to court for one client at 9:30 in the morning (I leave my office at 8:00 a.m.) and the judge calls my case at 12:30 p.m., I bill you from 8:00 a.m. to 12:30 p.m. (or 4 ½ hours of billable time), plus the return trip to my office. Now, if I bring other work with me and I do the other work while in court instead of sitting around doing nothing while waiting for my case to be called, I can bill as much as seven and one half hours total: four and one half billed to you and three billed to someone else. The situation is even rosier if I have several appearances in the same court-house for several clients on the same day.

In large law firms, if I am fortunate enough to be in a "reviewing" capacity at the firm, meaning I am a senior associate or junior partner, I can not only bill for my own work, but I can bill on top of the junior associates' work as well. Therefore, let us assume that I get to the end of the day and I have eleven hours billed on my own work. During the day, five junior associates submit their work to me for review. I can bill at least a fifteen minute increment (remember the .25 rule) on each item reviewed for each associate. This is the magic of large law firm billing. So if each associate gives me five items to review, I would bill 1.25 hours per associate (5 x .25) or 6.25 hours altogether (5 x 5 x .25). My total billable time for the day is now 17.25 hours. I have the makings of firm stardom.

Billing pressures and enormous overhead cause large law firms to disdain settlement. Large firms put up a brave front in regard to their cases. If they filed the suit, it has all the merit in the World and all the relief the client has demanded should be turned over at once. If it is their client who is sued, the case has no merit whatsoever, and should be dismissed with penalties awarded against the people who dared to instigate the suit. However, as much as the large firm demands an immediate surrender by the opposing side, this is exactly the opposite of what the firm really wants. In reality, large firms will do anything to avoid a settlement, or any type of quick resolution to a case. This is motivated primarily by the desire to keep cases around in the office as long as possible because each case represents an opportunity to bill. Large firms will recommend that their client fight a case which could be settled for $10,000.00, instead convincing the client to pay $200,000.00 in legal fees to defend the case. In essence, the law firm foments a dispute between its client and the other side, or, at a minimum, heightens the bad feelings between the adversaries. They have to do this because if they sat down with the other side and attempted to be reasonable (and the large law firm on the other side did the same), they might actually end up with an early settlement of the controversy. This, of course, would ruin the profits of both firms so we couldn't have that, now could we?

This should prompt one to ask: Who's stupid here? Every day of the week clients fight these cases, believing they are doing so on the basis of "principle" when the only principle involved is the desire of the large firm to make money. The best part of the story is that these clients come back to the same firm again and again for the same type of cost-ineffective representation. My experience has shown that up-front mediation can result in many settlements, saving clients tens of thousands of dollars (or far more) in needless legal expense.

The Type of Work Junior Associates handle

As a junior associate, you may rest assured, if the work is good, you won't get it for a few years. In my first year of practice, I was once called upon to litigate a case where I was defending a fan manufacturer on a claim that the fan had malfunctioned resulting in a "strange odor" emanating about the claimant's home. The claimant demanded $25.00 to settle the claim. We conducted an in-depth investigation into the claim, which included the client paying the firm about $500.00 in legal fees, and then the client ended up paying the claim in full anyway. I was also called upon to try a case where the firm's client had been sued for $50.00. I won the case after an extended trial so my client didn't have to pay $50.00 to the party who sued him. He did, however, have to pay the firm's bill which was in excess of $2,000.00. At the end of the day, he paid $2,000.00 instead of $50.00. So, did he really win the case?

The more significant cases my colleagues and I handled (in a loose sense) involved the product liability cases. When I first entered the insurance defense firm, I was designated to handle claims involving kerosene space heaters. I learned a lot more about kerosene heaters, how they work, and the fact that you would have to have your head examined to buy one, than I did about law. I also handled tractor cases and to some extent other products, like three wheel recreational vehicles. After a few years of handling such cases one becomes afraid to leave the confines of one's home. Actually, this is not completely accurate. One becomes afraid of one's home as well.

Working at an insurance defense firm, one must develop a sick sense of humor. I recall one of the partners defending a case where a man accidentally cut off a portion of his arm with a tree-trimming device. Our firm was representing the manufacturer of the device. One of the allegations of the complaint was that our device did not do what it was designed to do. This would be considered a "design defect" in the arena of product liability law. The partner advised the attorney for the plaintiff that he failed to see in what manner the device was defective. After all, it did precisely what it was supposed to do: It cut "limbs".

The same partner was handling a case where an entire family fell off a ski lift, injuring themselves. The husband, as is his right in New York State, asserted a claim for loss of his wife's companionship, services and consortium. This last item—available to married couples only—involves basically loss of or damage to a couple's sex life as a result of the personal injury to one or both spouses. In response to the plaintiff's demand of $500,000 for loss of the wife's consortium, the defense attorney asked the plaintiff's attorney if he could "try the wife out" because "nobody's worth $500,000".

The kerosene heater cases were a hot item around the office (I couldn't resist that one). Most of the cases involved people blowing themselves to bits, or burning themselves to a crisp by fueling the heaters with gasoline, instead of kerosene. To this day, I will not pump my own gasoline at the station. I always get a charge out of the service station personnel who smoke cigarettes while pumping your gas. Let the station attendant burst into flames, not me.

Some of the kerosene heater cases involved people falling on top of the heaters. Every so often you would get a twist. I recall one case where the family sealed the house up like a tomb: closing all windows tightly, shutting the door, and the like. They had the house hermetically sealed. Then they fired up the heater and left it running all night, or for all eternity as far as they were concerned. The house indeed became a tomb after all the oxygen dissipated. If I learned anything from these cases it was to stay away from fire or anything that burns: something I probably should have learned as a child.

Large law firms, as discussed above, disdain settlement. In short, they hate resolving cases. This is mostly because if the case resolves by settlement, the firm can no longer bill the file. But it also strikes at the collective ego of the firm that they have somehow been emasculated merely because the respective clients in a particular controversy have been able to strike a deal on some common ground. In a classic case of the large law firm missing the cue on settlement, we once had a case we were defending (or at least trying to defend) in the plaintiff-friendly jurisdiction of Detroit. The plaintiff had been burned to a crisp while working with a kerosene heater. To this day, we will never know what exactly this guy was doing with the heater, but it seemed to be a case of misuse. Nonetheless, your average Detroit jury sees a severely injured plaintiff and wants to pay him a lot of money: *your money.* We were within a mere $200,000.00 of settling the case. The plaintiff's attorney gave a final demand during the early part of the trial for $1,000,000.00. Our client thought this was a bit steep, based upon our firm's advice, so we offered $800,000.00 in settlement. The offer was rejected. Clearly, the case would have settled at $1,000,000.00, and it's a pretty good bet that it might also have settled at somewhere between $800,000.00 and $1,000,000.00 (such as $900,000.00?). As a result of the failure to settle, the jury subsequently opened up the field by awarding $6 million to the plaintiff.

The day the jury verdict came into the office, I found myself ordered by my superior to break the news to the client. As one would imagine, this was not a rewarding experience. Hello, Mr. Client. Remember that case we were $200,000 away from settling, well, guess what?

One of the more "intellectual" projects assigned to me was to research the effect of the Hague Convention (an international treaty dealing with how and where to serve suit papers on persons in other nations) on a British citizen being sued in the United States Courts. I recall spending many days researching all the intricate issues of service and then presenting the most senior partner in the firm with my results. When an associate is called to the office of a very senior partner, the look is that of a third grade student called to the principal's office. Somehow, someway, you feel as though you have done something wrong. You feel as transparent as a piece of glass. On this particular occasion, the very senior partner had two other senior partners in his office. He quickly surveyed my work and asked the one question I didn't think to research: whether or not Great Britain had ever signed on to the Hague Convention in the first instance. I couldn't answer. I crawled out of the senior partner's office on all fours.

A colleague handled mostly cases involving firework displays and the things that can go wrong with them. The general public attends a fireworks display and feels entirely safe and secure. You are there to enjoy the show. But if you've been handling product liability cases long enough, you find yourself ducking for cover even before the show starts. In one such instance, people were all gathered around watching a fireworks display when a rocket landed on top of a home, causing the roof to catch fire. A group of firemen were watching the blaze when one of them finally realized that it was his home ablaze. He ran off to fight the fire: by climbing a ladder and attempting to snuff the fire out with his bare hands. Needless to say, the fire raged on, and the fireman ended up in the hospital with second and third degree burns.

Another fine case involved a boat parade on a river in West Virginia. The junior attorney was brought in to attend a very serious meeting amongst the client (a fireworks manufacturer), partners of the law firm representing the manufacturer and expert engineers: the purpose of which was to investigate a fireworks display mishap. A film was shown in which old stern wheel-style boats were seen lazily cruising down a serene West Virginia river. Brilliant fireworks were seen exploding into the air: majestic colors of red, blue, yellow and green. All seemed well until suddenly the fireworks exploded on the boat rather than in the air, resulting in the boat doing an impression of the Titanic as it sank to the bottom of the river. People were shown in the film diving off the boat and into the water: all Hell breaking loose. The junior attorney is supposed to sit through such a film with a straight face.

This same junior associate was treated to yet another film involving a fireworks display that never got off the ground, in a manner of speaking. In this display, the fireworks technician forgot to secure the rack which holds the missiles for the show. This resulted in the missiles shooting out horizontally into the crowd, instead of vertically into the air. Once again, all Hell broke loose as people went scattering for cover. It was a virtual Armageddon. Again, no laughing permitted. No large law firm client wants an attorney with a sense of humor.

As a general rule, associates handle the type of work that the partners used to handle when they were associates. They didn't want to handle this work when they were younger and they certainly do not want to do it now. As a result, young associates rarely see the light of day. They are closeted in the law library[5] researching esoteric principles of law, or confined to their closet-sized offices drafting up papers that will be signed by someone more senior than them. My first "office", for lack of a better word, measured roughly six feet by nine feet: and I shared it with another attorney! I would have killed to have been permitted to set up my office in Paris Hilton's shoe closet.

Unless you have been at the large law firm for several years, you are permitted to sign nothing. The senior associates or the partners sign all the pleadings and motions and briefs and the like. I remember getting to the point where I was unconsciously signing my supervising partner's name to Valentine's cards, Christmas cards, my checkbook and the like. I could not even remember my own name. I still can't. I do, however, still remember my assigned attorney identification number from nineteen years ago: 1752. It is like a number emblazoned into my arm somewhat akin to the survivors of the Holocaust.

---

5.   Sometimes the law library can be fun. At the large law firm I was employed by, the firm maintained a librarian who must have been born around the same time as Abraham Lincoln. The librarian was nearly 100 years old and quite deaf. Associates at the firm would call down to the library and ask for persons to be paged: persons who obviously didn't work at the firm. Thus, the ancient librarian would receive a phone call, and would yell out to see if persons such as David Bowie, Michael Jordan, Bono, Mick Jagger and the like were available to take the call. If this librarian is still with the firm, the associates are probably still playing the same game with him. However, the names have most likely changed. Nowadays, I am sure that Christina Aguilera, Britney Spears and Diddy are some of the people supposedly working at the law firm.

Motions: a misnomer

The term "Motion" seems to indicate that something is about to be moved along, to wit, set in motion. In reality, motions generally serve to ensure that a case drags out longer than it is supposed to. Motions are primarily the tools of large law firms for prolonging cases and generating more billings, hence supplemental income for the firm.

There are many different types of motions. Some are what attorneys refer to as "substantive" motions, such as the summary judgment motion. The summary judgment motion essentially seeks a determination of the lawsuit on papers presented to the judge, in lieu of a trial. The summary judgment motion, if successful, will indeed deprive the loser of his so-called "Day in Court". Other motions are non-substantive, such as a motion to change the venue (place) of a trial from one county to another county. In personal injury actions in New York one often sees defense motions to change the venue of the trial to the so-called more "conservative" counties of Westchester, Putnam, Nassau, Suffolk and other defense-oriented counties. The defense firms try to get the personal injury cases into such conservative counties under the theory that no matter how badly injured the plaintiff is and no matter how badly negligent the defendant was, these jurors could care less. They will award the plaintiff nothing. In this instance, the defense attorneys are right.[6]

Filing motion after motion has become vogue with the large law firms because this is a perfectly acceptable method of generating excessive legal fees. The latest rave seems to be the motion to disqualify the other side's attorney from representation in the case. These motions are generally a pointless exercise, but the large law firms are filing them with more frequency. A motion to disqualify, if successful, essentially chucks the opposing attorney off the case. The usual purported reason for this is the supposed "conflict of interest" of the attorney sought to be discarded from the case. However, large law firms now routinely abuse the motion because the fact is that they simply don't want *anybody* representing their adversary.

---

6.   As an attorney trying a case on behalf of a plaintiff (or at least attempting to do so) in one of these conservative counties, you get some interesting remarks from potential jurors as you make your jury selection (referred to as "voir dire"). Jurors make statements such as: "Well, my brother was in a car accident once, but he didn't sue". "We don't believe in suing people". "We're not that type of people". As you can imagine, this does not give the plaintiff's attorney a very good feeling about his chance of success with such jurors.

The Non-Billable Project

These lovely items run the gamut from "legal" projects to the decidedly "non-legal". Large law firms tend to assign a good deal of what is generally referred to as "Non-Billable" work to the junior attorneys. For example, if a senior partner decides to author a treatise about some aspect of the law, it is a good bet that several junior associates have actually performed the back-up research, and in many instances, have actually written the treatise. The senior partner then becomes the accredited author of the work with little, if any, credit being given to the associate or associates who actually did the work. As one can imagine, this type of work takes plenty of time, especially since no junior attorney wants to be the one who submits an entirely inaccurate statement of the law to a publisher in the name of his boss. This can be absolutely fatal to the career objectives of the junior associate. Therefore, even though these ludicrous projects bring no money whatsoever into the firm, the junior associates tend to spend more time on these matters than they do on matters of more substance. The end result: no matter how many total hours the junior associate works, his or her "billable" hours will falter as a result of these non-billable projects. The standard firm line for these unfortunate associates is something along the lines of: "Well, we expect you nonetheless to maintain your billable hours in accordance with firm guidelines". This translates into: "We expect you to sleep less". So, the junior associates sleep less than the partners do. This is a guarantee at any large law firm. As a junior attorney, you will not sleep well. You will not be allowed to.

The non-legal, non-billable projects are generally less time-consuming but far more comical and humiliating. These range from picking up a senior partner's wife at the airport, to driving a senior partner's car to the repair shop, delivering Christmas gifts to clients, and the like. This type of work may not be precisely what you had in mind when you decided to attend law school.

Calendar Calls

Associates routinely handle court "Calendar Calls" when they first start out with a large firm. I could never understand why they refer to these creatures as calendar calls. They should really be "Cattle Calls". In New York practice, the courts are constantly calling the attorneys for the respective parties into court for "conferences" on pending cases. A conference was originally meant to get the attorneys on the case together with the assigned judge to discuss the merits of the case, investigate the possibility of settlement, and map out what pre-trial procedures will be employed in the case. The goal: either to settle the case or get it ready for trial. Unfortunately, these conferences have rather devolved into a series of meaningless trips to the courthouse to fill out form after form and then drop it into the hands of a clerk. Not a word about the merits of the case is exchanged. At these conferences, a judge is usually assigned for the duration of the case, or at least until such time as the clerks decide to re-assign the case to a different judge. The assigned judge typically has no familiarity whatsoever with the case. In fact, most often you don't even say one word to the judge when you appear for a "conference" on the case. Sometimes you don't even see the judge, because the judge is either not there or is sitting somewhere in his or her office (called "Chambers") having coffee and reading the newspaper. The clerks handle the calendar.

Nowhere is the cattle call more exemplified than in Kings County (Brooklyn), New York, where preliminary conferences encompassing at least two hundred cases are all scheduled simultaneously in one large room on the first floor of the courthouse. If we take into consideration the fact that each case must have at least two attorneys (and usually more), and multiply this by two hundred, we have roughly four hundred lawyers all crammed into a room at one time: all seeking the audience of one or two clerks. These clerks could generally care less if you have to spend the entire day sitting there waiting for your case to be called. The best part of the entire process is that a case is not called by the clerk until all attorneys on the case are present. Therefore, even if your case is number 1 on the calendar and you arrive at 9:30 a.m. as you are required to, you could conceivably wait until 2 o'clock in the afternoon just to speak with the clerk, if your adversary decides to show up late. On top of that is the fact that after all these hours you have wasted, nothing of substance has occurred. The case is no closer to a resolution than it was the day before. Next, you have to explain this to your client, who is being billed for six hours of your time for speaking with a clerk a total of 2 minutes.

The exception to the wait-in-line-all-day rule in Kings County and some of the other Boroughs of New York City is the attorney who knows the clerks well. This is the "legal line-cutter". I once had a case appear as the number one case on the court's calendar at 9:30 a.m. in Richmond County, New York (this is Staten Island). My adversary and I were both young attorneys so we showed up fifteen minutes early. It took me about 4 hours to get to Staten Island from my home in Connecticut so I had to get out of the house at 5:30 a.m. What followed during the next 3 1/2 hours was an endless parade of old-time, comically dressed Staten Island practitioners, each showing up at 10 o'clock, 11 o'clock and 12 noon: all of whose cases were called prior to ours. Each time one of these "old boys" entered the courtroom, the clerk, who had to be at least three hundred pounds, would immediately take these old boys off to see the judge. My adversary and I finally got in to see the judge just before 1 p.m. and we were soundly rebuked for being "late" for the calendar and for interfering with the judge's lunch.

The general rule is that if you have only a few cases in the courts of New York City you would be wise to hire a local practitioner to appear on your behalf: preferably one who has managed to ingratiate himself with the clerks who run the show. Otherwise, it could be a very long, painful day for you.

The end-result of the typical court conference is a check-a-box form filled out by the attorneys, and supposedly signed by a judge. The judges sign several hundred of these form orders at one time. The orders are all stacked up on the judge's desk or bench to sign. The judges could not possibly read all of these orders or, for that matter, even a small percentage of them. Instead, the judge's clerk usually stamps the judge's name or initials on the order. These orders contain deadlines for the attorneys to take certain actions in the case. This is of little consequence, however, since the attorneys routinely disregard the deadlines anyway. During the course of a case, numerous orders may be entered into by the attorneys—as the attorneys consistently miss previously ordered deadlines—and then signed off on by the very judges whose prior orders have been disobeyed.[7]

I think the ultimate oxymoron is the Connecticut calendar system which refers to itself as the "Short Calendar". The Short Calendar is Connecticut's version of the cattle call. As opposed to Kings County, New York, you have perhaps one hundred attorneys, but the calendar is every bit as slow, prompting one to

---

7.   Nowhere is the concept of routinely disobeying court discovery orders more rampant than in cases involving the City of New York. The City of New York is supposedly represented by its "Corporation Counsel", which consists of an appointed individual with the appropriate political ties, who rarely, if ever, sees the inside of a courtroom. Instead, the Corporation Counsel's office is filled with administrative personnel attempting to justify their existence, and extremely underpaid and miserable Assistant Corporation Counsels, who are the attorneys actually purporting to handle the cases filed against the City of New York. However, it is a tradition that while other parties are supposed to obey court discovery orders, the City of New York and its Corporation Counsel are permitted virtually free reign to disobey as many orders as they choose and to drag the resolution of cases out indefinitely. Simply put, the City of New York is accorded a favored status as a litigant. The Corporation Counsel's office even sets up shop, so to speak, in the courtroom in places that other attorneys would not be permitted to be. In one such city court, the Assistant Corporation Counsel actually sits in the witness box, next to the judge, during the call of the Calendar.

question who it is who came up with the term "Short Calendar". How can something be "short" if you end up sitting there doing nothing for hours?

The Large Law Firm Support Staff

A few words are required regarding the so-called "Support Staff" at law firms. The larger the firm, the greater the number of support personnel required to run the firm. The heart of the support staff is supposed to be the attorney's personal secretary. Hollywood tends to portray the secretary as the all around mother hen who shepherds the brilliant, but disorganized attorney through his or her day. The secretary provides moral support; reminds the attorney of all appointments; reminds the attorney about her son's little league game and to get a card for her husband's birthday. The personal secretary books flight arrangements, hotel accommodations, picks up lunch, advises the attorney if his tie isn't straight or his fly is not zipped shut.

All of the above is a perfectly true and accurate depiction of the lawyer's personal secretary. Hollywood finally got it right, that is, if we are talking about the *senior partner's* secretary.

Associates' secretaries are a completely different breed of cat. A junior associate usually finds that his or her first secretary can be a formidable adversary. My first personal secretary was offered to me to be shared with another associate whose head was one or two above mine from the bottom of the firm totem pole. This woman was at the tender age of 19 when she was hired as my secretary. She had no previous secretarial experience whatsoever and had little experience with a typewriter. Her phone skills consisted of yelling at clients and adversaries alike, and hanging up the phone on my friends and family. I would generally get my messages a day or two after the fact, unless I specifically asked her if anyone had called for me. The majority of my secretary's time was spent on the telephone engaged in hiring and firing catering halls, rock bands, disc jockeys, florists and the like for the wedding in which she was to marry an 18 year old boy, also fresh out of high school.

My dealings with my own secretary consisted of begging her to do my work, and having her curse at me anytime I asked her to do anything while she was planning her wedding. Of course, she was always planning or revising some aspect of the wedding, therefore I was relegated to the word processing pool (a shared group of typists) for most of my typed work. This actually turned out to my advantage since I became very friendly with one of the night typists, who subsequently introduced me to her sister, who has been my wife for the past 17 years.

All in all, I was fortunate: as little work as my secretary did for me, she actually did show up. And, she indirectly found me a wife.

A colleague was not so lucky. He and another associate were assigned a secretary who had a substance abuse problem and whose husband was serving a prison sentence. This secretary had a "stellar" attendance record. She was almost perfect. She almost never showed up to work. On the rare occasion when she did show up at work—very late—she would appear to be busy doing her work. However, unbeknownst to the two associates she worked for, she was secretly throwing their letters and correspondence in the garbage pail or hiding these items in the deep, dark recesses behind her desk. It was only after this secretary was finally fired that her desk was ransacked, revealing just why these two associates were always missing deadlines, court appearances, meetings with clients and the like.

Another colleague was assigned the psycho secretary. This secretary would scrape the paint off the walls on the opposite side of the hallway to stay as far away from human contact as possible. You could not get within ten feet of this secretary. The attorney could not hand anything to her. He had to drop papers onto her desk, and she would, in turn, drop the finished product back onto his desk. Anytime he approached her, she quickly backed away, or slid her chair as far away from him as possible: sometimes entirely to the opposite side of her cubicle. I don't know how he could stand it. But, then again, she showed up to work. She is most likely residing at the present time in a mental institution.

Sometimes you have to wonder where your secretary found his or her brain—if indeed he or she was ever given one. A colleague once had a secretary working for him who really should have gone with Dorothy and company to see the Wizard of Oz and, as the scarecrow did, requested a brain. The secretary was supposed to send a letter enclosing a litigation pleading (a complaint) to an insurance underwriter with the address, c/o Alexander Company, Bridge Street, London, England. The letter should have read something along the uncomplicated lines of: "Enclosed please find a copy of the complaint in this action". Instead, the secretary sent a letter to the London underwriter stating: "Please make sure the enclosed complaint is delivered to Alexander Hamilton[8] on the London Bridge".

Large law firm support staff is mind-boggling. Most large firms have more non-attorney staff than they have attorneys. Would you like to guess who supports this enormous, redundant infrastructure? That's right, the clients, via the

---

8.   The renowned American statesman, politician, financier and patriot who died in 1804.

associates' billings. The larger the law firm, the more non-attorney administrators. The more billing clerks, accounts receivable clerks, fax machine operators, secretaries, receptionists, night-typists, supply room clerks, mail-room sorters and delivery persons, etc. The more administration: the more paper-work for the associates. The more time spent on non-legal, administrative paper-work, the less time spent on billable matters. But the partners have a solution for this: it's called the weekend. This is when the partners play golf and the junior associates desperately attempt to catch up on their work: or at least meet their billable time quotas.

By now, I hope I have convinced you that large law firm life for the junior associates basically stinks.

Despite the foregoing, large law firms can be a wonderful opportunity for non-lawyers. Since large law firms have so many policies and persons to manage, these firms have plenty of administrative and bureaucratic positions to fill. Some of these positions are well compensated. But the best part of the job is that the rules which apply to the attorneys usually do not apply to the administrative personnel. So, if you are a computer analyst for the firm and you take a hankering to another young, attractive computer analyst, you are free to act as you see fit. The firm does not deem you a "professional", therefore the so-called ethics of the profession do not apply to you. Also: non-lawyers are not expected to work the night-shift, unless that is indeed their assigned work time, in which case they get to sleep during the day. These non-lawyer employees also do not have the pressure of minimum billings. All in all, the bureaucratic and administrative positions at the large law firms are filled with persons who generally could not muster the employment criteria required by the United States Postal Service. But for the salaries paid in relation to the work required it can be a very nice deal.

In summary, my advice to attorneys is this: if you don't like endless and meaningless policies, and you don't like pressure to bill, and you relish the thought of having some life outside of the practice of law, don't sign up with one of the large law firms. You'll never be happy[9]. However, if you are a non-lawyer, these firms can be a great place to work, make money and socialize.

Lateral move or forward pass

It is said that the grass is greener on the other fellow's lawn. Nothing could be further from the truth in the practice of law. Large law firms constitute a bounty for Lawyer Placement Specialists, commonly known as "Head Hunters". A head hunter is a person or organization which specializes in getting you out of the large law firm you are in and getting you a job at another large law firm. That is what head hunters do, and when they are successful (i.e., they make a placement), the head hunters make a lot of money doing it. They are essentially people brokers. The problem with head hunters is that they get paid regardless of whether or not the associate stays at the new firm for more than a very short period of time. Therefore, the head hunters could care less whether or not they have made an appropriate placement. In other words, if you were perfectly miserable at your first job, and you then become even more miserable at the next job, the head hunter still gets paid to place you there. Remember the Laws of Supply and Demand? Since junior associates are so miserable at the large law firms, they are always quitting these firms: usually to seek what they perceive to be greener pastures at other large law firms.[10] There is always a strong demand to replace these associates. After all, how do you row a ship without stout slaves chained to the oars? Well, the head hunters understand the Laws of Supply and Demand and as a result they achieve wealth. And, they don't have to deal with the pressures of practicing law.

---

9. A couple of years ago a now famous e-mail made the rounds at major law firms, as an associate announced his departure from the firm. The associate announced that he considered his new position as a "trophy husband", a "step up" and that he was "no longer comfortable working for a group largely populated by gossips, backstabbers and Napoleonic personalities." He went on to say: "In fact, I dare say that I would rather be dressed up like a piñata and beaten than remain with this group any longer…I wish you continued success in your goals to turn vibrant, productive, dedicated associates into an aimless, shambling group of dry, lifeless husks."

10. What they don't realize is that these large law firms are all the same. Leaving one large law firm for another large law firm is like the slave from the 1700's leaving one plantation owner to take up with another plantation owner. It may be a different plantation, and you may be harvesting different crops, but you are still a slave.

The tell-tale signs of the associate who is shopping himself or herself around the head hunter circuit are as follows:

1. The associate has been with his first law firm between 1 to 3 years;

2. The associate, out of the blue, starts taking lunchtime or starts taking time to run errands;

3. The associate starts walking around the office with a face that bespeaks of guilt, or a face that indicates he or she has done something wrong;

4. The associate starts dressing in a more formal manner;

5. The door to the associate's office is closed, especially at certain times during the day, such as early morning, late in the day or at lunchtime; and,

6. The associate speaks in whispers on the telephone, and then hangs up when a partner or more senior associate enters the room.

The tell-tale sign of an associate who has successfully landed a new job is the classic Cheshire cat grin. The associate now has an offer to leave the firm so he or she is ecstatic and perhaps feeling even a bit guilty about the unfortunate junior associate colleagues he or she is leaving behind. Of course, what he or she doesn't realize is that at the new firm he or she will remain a slave, as he or she was at the old firm. The associate will simply have a different master. As Pete Townshend once wrote: "Meet the new boss; same as the old boss." [11]

The major hassle of working with a head hunting firm is that the associate now has to squeeze interviewing in with his or her assignments doled out by the current firm. And, the interviewing must be done secretly. The topic of interviewing could constitute an entire course. However, I thought I would share the following interview horror stories with you.

A colleague once had an interview with a prestigious old law firm located in Rockefeller Center, New York. This was the type of firm where none of the partners seems to have a first name, to wit, F. Lee Bailey, A. Martin Smith, S. Robert Johnson, and the like. This always caused me to wonder what happened to these persons' first names. Other partners in these "White Shoe", "Blue Blood" or "Silk Stocking" firms, as they are sometimes referred to, have names more akin to places than persons. Why on Earth would a parent name his son, for example, H. Cheshire Wellington? Or F. Cambridge Lounsbury, III? Can you imagine suffer-

---

11. The Who's: "Won't Get Fooled Again".

ing through life with these names? These are the type of firms where one can hear a pin drop at the busiest time of a work day. The only semblance of noise is the soft, but steady tap of the secretaries' quiet keyboards and the occasional muted ring of a telephone. All in all, the air reeks of sterility.

On the day of the interview, my colleague made sure to have his best dark suit dry-cleaned and ready to go. It was winter-time so he also made sure to wear his finest overcoat. As he took the elevator up to the main reception area of the firm, he noticed for the first time that he was indeed wearing his fine overcoat, and his best monogrammed shirt, tie and wing-tip shoes. However, he was not wearing his suit-jacket. He promptly accepted the hint the Universe was sending him and took the elevator back down to street level. He never took the interview.

I once interviewed at the same firm. I recall sitting for an eternity in the reception area waiting to be whisked off to some suffering junior associates' offices, where I was to hear them regale me with tales of their love for the firm and the work they did. Of course, all of these persons looked as though they hadn't slept in months. While in the reception area I couldn't help noticing the manner in which each attorney would enter the firm. In order to enter the firm one had to pass the receptionist, who was an older, prima donna looking, and perfectly coifed woman. As each attorney entered the firm, the receptionist would state "Good morning, Mr. Whiteside", to which the attorney would respond "Good morning, Ms. Pettibone". "Good morning, Mr. Uppington", "Good morning, Ms. Pettibone". After about forty-five minutes of this side-show, and my conferences with the associates, I was finally brought before a partner. This fellow mostly reminded me of Renfield, from the old Dracula films. I remember saying something witty, borderline funny, actually. This partner gave me a look as though I had poisoned him. My attempt at humor had clearly caused him physical pain. I decided against my continued pursuit of employment with this firm. That was okay, the firm felt the same way about me.

If one can get past the dress code requirements (a gentleman must wear his suit-jacket to an interview) and the preliminary interview, one may be called back for a second interview. The chief element of the second or "call-back" interview is that you must have lunch with members of the firm. This is about as fun as sticking needles in one's eyes.[12] You have to somehow figure out a way to eat while you yourself are essentially the main course. You are grilled with ridiculous questions throughout the meal. Questions such as; "So where do you see yourself five years from now? What do they expect you to answer them. "Well, I certainly do

---

12.   As Jack Nicholson said in the 1983 film "Terms of Endearment".

not see myself at this firm five years from now. I was actually intending to use your firm as a stepping-stone to something better." What you really want to say to the interviewer is: "I was hoping to win the lottery in the next year or so, and if I do the first thing I am going to do is quit this lousy job."

But the trickiest part of lunch is to make sure you order the correct food. Italian food can be disastrous because no matter how careful you are you will inevitably end up with red sauce on your white shirt or with olive oil on your tie. After the lunch, you have to go back to the firm and continue interviewing with other partners, so you have to make sure you remain clean. A good friend took an interview with one of the white shoe firms in Manhattan. He committed the cardinal sin of ordering dessert. This is always a mistake. He ordered blueberry pie. When he returned to the firm, he noticed that each person with whom he interviewed would speak with him for a few minutes and then asked to be excused, following which he would be shuttled to another partner's office. After several of these interviews he began to get the impression that there was chuckling following him from office to office. He excused himself to the mens' room and looked in the mirror: his teeth and tongue were blue.

He was not called back for a further interview.

5

The Small Firm: fewer hours, less pressure and other fallacies

You have finally decided to leave the large firm and to cast your fortunes with a smaller firm. You figure that you have a better chance of making partner at the smaller firm, and you will work less hours, and be less pressured for billings. Of course, you have had to take a substantial salary cut to make this change. But, you hope to regain your sanity, and perhaps see some of the hair grow back, which fell out at your old desk at the large firm.

Small firms can be summarized fairly simply. They are essentially identical to the large firms with the exception that they have less members; have smaller office space; and, have fewer policies. Other than that, they are essentially the same as the large firms. The small firm is run by the senior partners, who take home the overwhelming majority of the money the firm brings into its coffers. Small firms have fewer policies because there is simply less going on to have policy about. For example, it doesn't make much sense to have a policy about how to deal with Japanese clients when your firm doesn't do any business outside of the state in which it is located.

The so-called "Partnership Track" is undoubtedly shorter at the small firms than at the large firms. Therefore, if it takes eight to ten years to be considered for partnership at the large law firm, it most likely takes one half that amount of time to be considered for partnership at the small firm. There is, however, usually one catch. Small firms have a tendency to be, for lack of a better word, "intimate". It is not unusual for all of the partners in a small firm to be directly related to each other: the grandfather founded the firm, the father is the senior partner in the firm, and the junior partners are his sons and nephews. To make matters worse, most, if not all, of the associates in the firm (remember, these are the attorneys who are not yet partners but who are trying to be) seem to have the same last name or hyphenated middle name (in the case of the women) as the senior partner. This should give the unrelated new associate a good idea about his or her chances of making partner in the firm. The bottom line: small law firm advancement is primarily based upon nepotism and cronyism. You must either be a member of the club by birthright or you must figure out a way to break into the club, and do so quickly. Otherwise, you will spend the rest of your life as a poorly compensated and over-worked associate.

6

The Partner: Profit-Sharing and other Fairy Tales

Breaking out of the law firm environment altogether gives one a feeling of instant exhilaration. You are finally free. You will make the rules. You are the master of your own destiny. No more firm policies. No more ass-kissing. No more sucking up to the senior partner, his wife, his children, nephews and nieces. No longer will you pace about your cubicle during the December holidays wondering if you have been "made partner", or wondering if and how much of a bonus you will be doled out. From here on in, you will eat what you kill. And being a seasoned war veteran, you are ready to slay and rend. You and your partner will fight the good fight together to the end. You will be friends in glorious battle. Let's get rich together! Or so you think.

There is only one little problem with your plan: *the man (or woman) on the other side of the office.* This fellow has very different ideas. He shares your desire to succeed and to get rich. But he has other very different ideas about just how to achieve that goal. It would seem logical to assume that in a two person partnership, each partner performs roughly one half of the work for approximately one half of the compensation. In a perfect World, each partner would work roughly the same number of hours (with the same level of intensity), and each partner would enjoy about the same amount of vacation time.

Partnerships in the law, however, have a tendency to be as predatory as the profession itself. Small law firm partnerships break up with great frequency, and when they do, the Court system is generally flooded with acrimonious litigation lasting longer than the partnership itself was in existence. Large law firms very rarely dissolve. Instead, they suffer partner defections. Partner defections come in two types. The first type of defection is somewhat akin to the New York Yankees offering a contract to a free agent Red Sox player, such as Johnny Damon. The partner is simply made a better offer to work for the competing law firm, so away he or she goes. This then raises the interesting issue of attorney-client privilege and conflict of interest. The large multi-state and multi-national law firms invariably represent clients who are at odds with each other, such as Sun Microsystems and IBM or Microsoft. What happens when the partner, who has handled cases for Sun against Microsoft, now takes a position with the law firm which represents Microsoft? The new law firm will erect the proverbial "Chinese Wall" around the incoming partner. This means that the incoming partner may not have any dealings with Microsoft or Sun matters and may not have any discussions with any of the other attorneys at the new firm pertaining to these matters. Does the Chinese Wall work? I don't know. Ask the Chinese.

The second type of large firm defection is the en masse defection, where a group of disgruntled partners from one firm leaves to join another firm, or leaves to form their own firm. Sometimes senior associates will join the defectors as partners in the new firm, or with the promise that they will soon become partners in the new firm.

Large firm defections have a tendency to make the newspapers that attorneys read. However, these defections are not nearly as interesting as the small firm break-ups. This is because small law firms tend to be like marriages. You see the same faces every work day of the week for eight to twelve hours each day. You know how your partner likes his or her coffee. You know that at a certain time each day, your partner will stink up the office with his garlic-laden lunch. You know that at 5:30 pm each day after the secretary goes home, your partner will get up, walk to his cabinet, pull out the Jack Daniels and take a swig. You can finish your partner's sentences and he can finish yours. You know each other too well. It's like a marriage. And, when it breaks up, it can be as acrimonious as any divorce: or worse since you are both lawyers.

A colleague of mine set up a partnership with a friend from law school: the notorious two-person partnership. Statistics demonstrate that more than half of these two-person partnerships break up within one year of their formation. This partnership lasted less than three years. The basic problem with small partnerships is that the future partners generally do not discuss and agree upon the essential issues of the partnership arrangement in advance of setting up shop. Law partners become preoccupied with issues such as: where will the new firm get its business? What type of business will the firm get? Are we set up to handle such work? Are we familiar with the areas of the law which will require our expertise? How will we get paid? What will our overhead be? Can we get credit from a lender? Where will we set up our office? Where will we find a secretary? Which partner's name will go first on the letterhead? Who will print our stationery? Which color sofa goes best in our waiting room?

What the future partners rarely, if ever, discuss, is: how do we define profit and what do we do with the "Profit" once we get it? Once again, lawyers typically put "Law" before economics, which I have already demonstrated to be a mistake.[1] Why? *If you haven't figured it out by now, wealth is not about "Law", it is about Economics.*

The future partners assume, perhaps naturally, that since there are two partners, the profits will be divided evenly = 50/50. The future partners make plenty of assumptions, but they never actually get around to drawing up a partnership agreement spelling out who is going to do what or how they will be paid. The genesis of the problem is that law schools do not train future attorneys to concern themselves with issues as petty and mundane as money. After all, law is a profession, not a business: So one is taught in law school. Law schools are generally embarrassed by any discussion of money. It is ironic that money is a taboo subject at law schools: because money is pretty much the only issue practicing lawyers talk to each other about. It does not take too long for the newly-admitted attorney to come to the stark realization that the law is indeed a business like anything else.

So our two partners now embark on their new venture. They start up the practice in May and all seems well. The partners concentrate on finding new clients and selling these clients on their services. All is well until one of the partners decides to take a three week vacation: after being in business for two months. The partner left alone in charge of the office thinks this rather odd, but it's like a new marriage. He figures this is an aberration and the partners are good friends, so who cares?

However, after one lousy year in business and approximately three months worth of vacations for the one partner, and 1 week's vacation time for the other, the partnership becomes rather strained. Suffice it to say that the entire partnership worked this way. Obviously, these partners forgot to discuss the issue of vacation time prior to entering into the partnership. One partner simply assumed that vacation time would be the standard two weeks per year, or less for a new

---

1.   This comes from the lawyer's training. Law schools never want to approach the topic of money. Money is absolutely taboo in the realm of legal academia. It is, as they believe, beneath them. Consequently, the law is never referred to as a "business" in academic circles. It is referred to as a "profession". It is ironic that money is never discussed in law school since this is the main reason (sometimes the only reason) people attend law school.

business. The other partner apparently assumed that as a self-employed person he could take whatever amount of vacation time he wanted to take.

Another issue arose between the partners. The "vacationing partner" as we shall call him and the "working partner" as we shall call him never discussed the issue of how the work would be apportioned between them or how the money would be distributed. The working partner went into the business under the assumption that the partners would each spend approximately 50% of their respective time working on partnership business and would hence receive approximately 50% of the profits each. In addition to the extremely excessive vacation time, the working partner never anticipated that when the vacationing partner was actually physically present in the office he would not actually be working on clients' files. In fact, the vacationing partner was conducting his own real estate business for roughly 90% of his "work" time at the office. To compound matters, the vacationing partner was the owner of the building in which the law firm practiced, therefore he was receiving rent from the law firm partnership in addition to his receiving 50% of the profits of the partnership. Thus, in the very first year of the business the vacationing partner was physically present at the office for 9 months, and actually worked about 10% of that time: while making most of the money.

If the foregoing were not bad enough for our "working" partner, the vacationing partner was left alone in charge of the check-book as well as all books and records. The working partner had himself so embroiled in actually handling clients' cases and files that he did not take the time or effort to handle the administrative work. The vacationing partner, on the other hand, had nothing but time on his hands, so he was more than happy to handle the accounts, and write the checks. Unfortunately for our working partner, most of the checks were written to—you guessed it—the vacationing partner.

As you can imagine, it was a very pleasant situation for the vacationing partner until the working partner finally came to his senses, realized he was being fleeced and hired his own attorney to break up the partnership. Another two—person partnership bites the dust.

The moral of the story is simple: When you assume, you make an ass out of you and me. If you are going to set up a small firm partnership, sit down, figure out every aspect of partnership life, agree on it, and *then put it in writing*. If you can't agree on essential issues, then you probably weren't meant to be partners in the first place. You are better off knowing this up front, rather than later in court: or with your hands clenched around your partner's throat (which has been known to happen).

7

Going it alone: Self-Determination or Self-Destruction?

You have now reached the point of no return. You have worked for too many firms. You have had a failed partnership. You are virtually unemployable. You are damaged merchandise. You are like an un-chaste woman in a fundamentalist Islamic nation. No one will touch you. You have no choice but to go it on your own because no one else will hire you. This is underscored by the fact that you cannot even get an interview; and, no head-hunting firm worth its salt will touch you. You shudder at the thought of re-training: going back to school to obtain an MBA degree or to study computers. It's too late for these things, not to mention the fact that you are broke and the bills are piling up. You are in the position you always dreaded: you have become a lawyer by default. Leaving the profession is no longer an option.

You attempt to hide your sheer terror (of poverty, or worse, having to crawl back to your former employer on hands and knees and beg for your old job back), by becoming artificially excited about starting up your own solo practice. You spend time, and money you do not have, at print shops and stationeries ordering impressive letterhead and business cards. You begin attending functions which would have made you cringe as a teenager. Democratic functions; Republican functions; Conservative, Liberal; Pro-Life; Pro Choice: you are not discriminatory. You have become a chameleon: you can be whatever they want you to be at the drop of a hat. You assist with campaigns of persons you don't even know, proudly endorsing these candidates to the general public. You attend Rotary Clubs, Lions Clubs, Elks Clubs, and every community, religious and civic organization you can think of. By this time, you have attended more dull functions than you would care to remember. You have eaten plenty of runny eggs and rubber chickens at these dull networking breakfasts and luncheons. You have even degraded yourself further by soliciting your own parents and their friends for business. You are one step away from standing on the street wearing a 2-sided placard to advertise your legal services. And, then the first client comes along.

The first client is invariably the friend of a friend or a relative. After several years of self-employment one learns never to represent family members, no matter how distantly related, and rarely, if ever, to represent friends. Friends and relatives typically view attorneys the way most of the general public does. They believe that you are fabulously wealthy and for this reason you don't need to charge them for your work. Besides, you owe them a "good deal" because they are family. Prior to setting up your own practice, nobody wanted to associate with you. However, you now find every second cousin three times removed knocking at the door seeking free legal advice. In addition to not paying you, family and friends have a tendency to call incessantly, thereby preventing you from getting any paying work done. Friends and family also have no qualms about calling you at home at un-Godly hours of the night or on the rare occasions when you are supposed to be on vacation.

When one starts out as a sole practitioner, one takes any case that walks in the door. All that is required of a potential client is a pulse. After some time, you invariably end up wishing you could get rid of most, if not all, of the cases you took when you first started out. But you can't just get out. You are not allowed to quit. One of the problems with the legal profession is the inability to get out of a bad deal. For example, if an electrician makes a bad deal with a homeowner, the electrician will simply abandon the job and move onto something more profitable. The same holds true for plumbers and other tradesmen, who tend to disappear from jobs they committed themselves to in order to pursue better jobs. Have you ever wondered why the plumber, who started but did not finish your toilet repair job on Monday, disappeared entirely, refusing to return your phone calls, after a days' work? What occurred was this: after you hired the plumber, he received a call to handle a much larger and more lucrative job. Thus, he simply abandoned your small job in favor of the larger, more profitable job. Of course, if a plumber starts your project, and you fail to pay him, he will also abandon your project ...—And, rightfully so.

This ability to move from job to job based upon profitability (or lack thereof) does not apply to attorneys. Once an attorney has entered an appearance on behalf of a client in a court matter, the attorney simply cannot unilaterally get out of the matter, *even if the client refuses to pay him*. No matter how bad the deal is, the attorney cannot get out of the case. There are only two options available to the attorney. One is to ask the client to terminate the attorney's services and obtain a so-called discharge.[1] The problem with this avenue of relief is that if the client is smart enough, he will not discharge his attorney. Why should he? He knows that the attorney will have to continue working on his case even though he is not being paid. As a sole practitioner, you discover that there is an entire market of "professional clients" out there who are masters of coercing and conniving attorneys into taking cases and then locking the attorneys into these cases, free of charge. The only other method of securing release from bondage is for the attorney to make an application to the court seeking to be "relieved" of his or her obligation to represent the non-paying or uncooperative client. The problem here is that the client has the opportunity to oppose the application, and the courts do not always grant these applications in any event: even if the application receives no opposition (or objection). Rest assured, if the application is made too close to an upcoming trial date, the court will deny the application and force the attorney to try the case—without payment. Sounds impossible? It happens more often than you would think. The moral of the story is that if a client slows down on paying legal fees, the attorney is rewarded for moving quickly to dump the case and get rid of the client. However, if the attorney tries to stay with the client and tries to work things out amicably with the client, the attorney is penalized by potentially getting locked into the case. And, there is a bumper crop of so-called "professional" clients who are well aware of this and know how to play it to their advantage: all the while feigning their naivete and poverty.

While on the topic of non-paying clients, a word is in order about "Pro Bono Publico" work. Literally translated, this means "for the public good". Large law firms love pro bono work because such work is inexpensive from a person-power standpoint and is not only good advertising for the large firm, but also serves to further the political aspirations of the partners. For example, a firm might be very much on the side of the so-called pro choice activists, in which case the firm will assign several associates to perform research and submit what are referred to as "Amicus Curiae" (this means literally "Friend of the Court") briefs to the United States Supreme Court and other federal courts in support of this position. Another firm might be on the side of the so-called Pro Lifers, and this firm would do much the same thing going the other way. When all is said and done, the pro bono project draws attention to the firm's work: which is precisely what the firm and its partners wanted in the first place. Remember also that these large law firms can push this work off as additional non-billable projects to their junior

---

1.   In other words, the attorney is in the bizarre position of having to ask the client to fire him or her.

associates. As we discussed earlier, these junior associates can make up their lost billable time on the weekends.

Mandatory pro bono work for the sole practitioner, on the other hand, is nothing shy of a violation of the United States Constitution's Thirteenth Amendment proscription against involuntary servitude (also known as slavery). You learn in law school that no person may be coerced into working free of charge, to wit, as a slave. However, you find out in the profession that pro bono work by attorneys is the exception to the rule.

You are a sole practitioner. Your daily routine revolves around desperately attempting to squeeze out the paper-work required for your practice; preparing for and making your court appearances; trying to avoid the incessant telephone calls from clients; trying to develop the ability to be in two or sometimes even three places simultaneously; and, above all things, trying to get yourself paid: All the while trying to cope with the myriad non-billable, administrative requirements placed upon you by the Office of Court Administration as they refer to it in New York State ("OCA" for short). In the midst of the usual daily chaos, you show up at the office one day to find a letter from the administrative judge's office, which includes an order in a case you do not recognize. You do not recognize the case because you represent neither the plaintiff nor the defendant. Wrong!

You read on. You now find out, much to your chagrin that you have been ordered by the administrative judge, to immediately drop everything you are doing and commence representation of one of the parties to the lawsuit. You are specifically directed that you may not charge this client for your work because you have been assigned to represent this client on a pro bono basis. The typical pro bono case is a twisted, contorted matrimonial action where a husband and wife who have nothing whatsoever to fight about are fighting nonetheless. You don't even know how to handle a matrimonial case. You know nothing at all about this area of the law. But, the court system has placed you into a case where you have no desire to be; representing a client you would never in your right mind represent; and, you must donate your time for free to do it. Rest assured, there will be no compensation for the time you have lost in not being able to service other clients. Moreover, there are most likely more immediate, upcoming dates with respect to your new case, so you now have to start juggling around your paying clients and cases to handle the case for the non-paying client: So much for the constitutional prohibition against involuntary servitude.

I have often wondered why pro bono publico work is limited to the legal profession. I recently had a plumber give me an estimate of $7,500.00 for some work to be done in my home. Since I did not have an extra $7,500.00 lying around, and since I had figured the job could not possibly have cost more than $3,000.00, I had to decline awarding the job. Why doesn't the court system order plumbers to handle jobs on a pro bono basis? In theory, there is no legitimate reason why not. If a court can order an attorney to handle a case free of charge, why can't the same court order an electrician to wire your hot-tub for free? What about accountants or physicians?

I suppose since the protections afforded citizens by the Constitution's Thirteenth Amendment do not apply to attorneys, why should the protections afforded by other federal laws apply to attorneys? An upstate New York bankruptcy judge recently held that the protections afforded by the United States bankruptcy laws did not apply to an attorney who, distraught with the legal profession, abandoned the profession and relocated to France. If one were ever considering attending law school, this tale would certainly dissuade one from doing so.

An obviously bright, energetic young man graduated college with a degree in psychology, philosophy and anthropology, before deciding to attend law school. Following his law school graduation, he entered the profession as a sole practitioner where he picked up cases from a legal defense program, as well as other criminal defense cases and civil rights cases. The law school tab consisted of $150,000.00 in student loans. After five years of practicing law, this gentleman never earned more than $33,000.00 in any given year. In the year 2000, he finished successfully defending himself in two malpractice claims, after which he found that his insurance premiums had risen so dramatically he could no longer afford malpractice insurance. During the same time period, the attorney's father's business was robbed, resulting in the attorney losing the desire to handle criminal defense work.

Fed up with the whole thing, the attorney closed his practice, filed for bankruptcy and then took off for France, hoping that his massive student loans and other bills would not follow him. The attorney contended that he was "not even qualified to be a street sweeper" in France and that he had no means of repaying the loans. The bankruptcy court refused to discharge the student loans holding that there are other career opportunities available to the attorney as a result of his education, training and experience. Of course, these "other" opportunities were not specified by the court.

The end result is a young person who has no desire whatsoever to practice law since he has never made any real money doing so, but may be forced to do just that in order to pay off the loans he had to take out just to go to law school.[2]

Clearly, getting paid by your clients (and, as you will see infra, client communications) is the bane of the sole practitioners' existence. However, the life of the sole practitioner is filled with other joys as well. In the large law firms there is an administrative person who handles practically everything from filing papers in court for the attorneys, to keeping track of the attorney's calendar, making travel arrangements, hiring investigators, process servers, court reporters and the like. In the large law firms there is someone assigned for each type of so-called "non-legal" or "administrative" work required in the practice. The sole practitioner, however, must do all of these things himself or herself. This is why most sole practitioners will go to the ends of the Earth to find a reliable, trustworthy and competent secretary and then do anything required to keep that secretary happy and on the job.

There are, however, a growing number of sole practitioners who believe that they can handle all aspects of the job themselves.[3] These are the attorneys who practice out of post offices boxes, out of their homes or out of their automobiles. These attorneys rarely answer the telephone and rely either on an answering service, or on the plain old, low technology answering machine. These attorneys sometimes have nothing but a cellular telephone number at which to reach them.

These attorneys must file their own documents, photocopy their own papers, type their own documents, and do everything including licking the envelopes. This type of practice, while undoubtedly a bare bones approach to the concept of overhead, can result in a premature nervous breakdown. *I should know, I am one of these attorneys.*

---

2. Another attorney, after practicing almost twenty years with a large law firm was told in no uncertain terms that he would never be elevated to partnership, nor would he ever receive another pay raise. He therefore embarked on his own. After two years of sole practice, he had his car repossessed in the wee hours of the night for non-payment. He could no longer obtain credit from any bank. He could not even get a credit card. He had no health insurance, no life insurance and no malpractice insurance. His teeth were falling out due to his inability to pay a dentist. In short, he and his wife were living hand-to-mouth. So don't be surprised if the guy on the street holding a tin cup and begging for your change was at one time your attorney.

3. A colleague, who is also one of these do-it-all-yourselfers, once decided to handle his own investigation into the scene of an accident. The attorney went to the south Bronx, where the accident occurred and proceeded to take photographs of the accident site, when a vagrant stopped and asked him what he was doing. When my colleague replied that it was none of the gentleman's business, the vagrant walked across the street, pulled down his pants and mooned the attorney: So much for the dignity of the profession.

8

The Client: Friend or Foe?

After 21 years in the legal profession, I can say without a doubt that one's own clients usually end up becoming your worst nightmare. But they can also provide you with the best source of madcap humor. Ask any practicing attorney what the most difficult aspect of the practice is and he or she will invariably respond: "Practicing law would be easy if it weren't for the clients".

Clients come in all shapes, colors and sizes, but they all have one thing in common: each client believes that his or her case is the only case the attorney is handling at any given time or that his or her case should be the only case the attorney is handling. Perhaps this misconception comes from a complete misunderstanding of just how attorneys make money. *With very few exceptions, attorneys make money by handling a large volume of cases.* The most obvious exception would be the now-deceased Johnny Cochran or the F. Lee Baileys of the World, who can, and will, spend a year or more on a very large case, and work on nothing else. But let's face facts: let's say you are a person who is very much in the public spotlight; you have substantial assets; and, you want to beat the rap one way or the other. You hire the Johnny Cohran type of attorney to represent you in your criminal trial. You pay him an up-front retainer of $500,000.00 to $1 million. You can certainly expect to call the attorney and speak with him on a daily basis about your case. And, the attorney will be happy to take your call. With this amount of money in-hand, why shouldn't he be happy to speak with you?

The problem is that the vast majority of the cases handled by most attorneys are in the small to mid-sized range. These are civil cases where the "real value" of the suit is anywhere between $5,000.00 to perhaps $300,000.00, regardless of whether the attorney represents the plaintiff (the person doing the suing) or the defendant (the person being sued). In the criminal arena, most cases run from the simple misdemeanor (such as driving while intoxicated first time offenders) to low level felonies, where the real chance of incarceration in excess of 1 year is slim to none. Since an attorney can't really justify an entire year's gross income on any one of these small to mid-sized cases, the attorney survives by taking on a substantial volume of such cases. The bottom line is that attorneys tend to take on a lot of work: usually more than they can legitimately handle. This is why the attorney cannot afford to have daily contact with any one particular client. If you are a client, I can assure you that your attorney is not working on your case every day of the week. He does not think about your case every day, as you do. He can't. He has another 200 cases he is also handling just like yours.

Representing clients is made particularly difficult by another basic misunderstanding about the role the attorney is supposed to be playing in the relationship between lawyer and client. It's really a no-win situation. Here's an example. If you want to build a house, you know that you are going to have to pay plumbers, electricians, carpenters, roofers and the like. When you pay the carpenter, you can actually see the walls, floors and windows of your new home. When you pay the plumber, you can see the furnace, air conditioning units and bathroom fixtures. You hire an electrician and you have light. You see something tangible for the money spent. No so with lawyers.

Clients approach lawyers because they have some sort of problem. If they didn't have a problem they wouldn't call a lawyer. Someone has sued you. Thus, you have a problem which has been foisted upon you. You want to sue someone else because you believe that someone has harmed you in some way. You want to purchase a property (home, business, real estate or personal) but you fear that you will not get what you bargained for. You want to sell something, but you want to make sure that you receive everything you are entitled to. You are accused (rightfully or wrongfully) of committing a crime; and you want to avoid the punishment. You want to work out an estate plan so that your family can obtain as much money as possible when you die, and the government will siphon off as little money as allowable. Your spouse has sued you for divorce. You have sued your spouse for divorce. One way or another, people come to lawyers because they have a problem.[1] Lawyers do not create the bad situation the prospective client finds himself or herself in. The client or someone else has already done that. For example, the matrimonial client has already siphoned off all the money from his or her spouse's bank accounts—and spent it all—before the client hires you. The person who was injured in an automobile accident decided not to see a physician

---

1.   Lawyers, of course, sometimes tend to make situations worse by becoming the problem. This is discussed in more detail in Chapter Twelve: "Your Own Lawyer: Friend or Foe?"

for six months after the accident—he decided to live with the pain. The person who caused the accident decided to ignore a stop sign just before the accident. The seller of the business is well aware of potential toxic waste beneath the property he wants to sell: his business caused it. The examples are myriad. The point is that the attorney did not create whatever bad situation exists for which the client seeks representation. The attorney is, in essence, stuck with the facts he or she is given to work with.

Nonetheless, one way or the other, the client seeks "Justice". To the client, "justice" means that the client wins and the other guy loses: regardless of who is right or wrong. From the client's perspective, if the client wins the case, justice was served, and he believes "Why do I need to pay an attorney simply because I was finally given what I deserved all along?" Of course, if the client loses the case, the desire to pay the attorney is even less (if not non-existent), even if the case could not possibly have been won by any style of creative legal wrangling. *The bottom line is that unlike the house-building example above, the client never feels he or she is getting anything of value for the legal fee paid, therefore the client never wants to pay the attorney.* Clients do not understand that it is not the lawyer's job to magically convert a bad situation into a good situation or to guarantee a win, regardless of the situation. The lawyer works within the framework of the facts given to him or her by his or her client. Win or lose, if the attorney does everything in his or her power, within the law, to obtain a victory for the client, the attorney has done his or her job. For this, the attorney deserves to be paid: win or lose. Lawyers attempt to solve the problems of their clients but they cannot guarantee the result.

Ironically, physicians, who generally hate attorneys, fail to realize that they have this important point in common with their fellow professionals. Physicians attempt to "repair" people, for lack of a better word, but sometimes no matter what they do, they cannot achieve the result. For example, the 70-year old man who has been smoking three packs of cigarettes each day for 50 years, and drinking hard liquor for the same amount of time, may very likely die during the open heart surgery to repair his severely damaged arteries, but is this the surgeon's fault? Physicians, like attorneys, toil within the framework of what they are given to work with. They try to solve problems; they do not guarantee to do so.

A plumber, on the other hand, will indeed guarantee a working sink and toilet, and if these things do not work, the plumber must ensure that they do. Other professionals such as electricians, carpenters, roofers, engineers and the like will indeed guarantee to solve problems. Lawyers will not. For example, if a person hires a roofer, the roofer will give him a price and a guarantee that if the client pays the price the roof will not leak for a certain period of time. However, when a client hires an attorney, he is given no guarantee that the money paid by the client will bring about the intended result. This is a very important point of friction between the attorney and the client, and, in my opinion, this friction cannot be *resolved*. It can be *explained* to the client, but it can never be eliminated altogether. The attorney's services, like that of the physician, come with no guarantee of success. This sets the attorney (and the physician) apart from almost every other conceivable contractual relationship between people.

Another major problem is the pricing of attorney's fees. The attorney can rarely give an exact price for his or her services. For example, would you buy a television set if the seller told you the set would probably cost $1,500.00, but the price could ultimately be a lot higher, and the set may or may not work? This is an essential difficulty in selling legal services. Clients do not know what exactly it is that they are buying and they do not know what the ultimate price will be.[2]

The inability to give a fixed price in the handling of a legal matter is most prominent in the handling of a civil or criminal litigated case. The attorney simply does not know at the outset of the case how much time he or she will ultimately end up spending on the case. The adversary could simply roll over and play dead, or the adversary could create enormous amounts of work for you. The court system could see things your way, or it could make the attorney jump through hoops. The case could settle early on or it could drag on to a lengthy trial and even post-trial appeal. It simply cannot be predicted. Clients hate this uncertainty. Wouldn't you?

As stated above, clients hire lawyers because they have problems. Sometimes clients have more "problems" than meet the eye.

Here are some of my favorite client "problem" stories.

The Tale of Mr. Johnson: I have found the landlord-tenant area of practice to be a fertile ground for insanity and mad-cap adventures. First and foremost is the story of Mr. Johnson. This gentleman owned a home which he and his wife were renting out to tenants who were slightly delinquent in their rental payments. The tenants were habitually several weeks to a month behind in their payments. Within a short time, it became obvious to me that Mr. Johnson was a bit "off". I

---

2.   One of the rare instances in which attorneys will "cap" a fee or offer a "fixed price fee" is in the area of real estate closings. Even unsophisticated clients shop around for price, usually by telephone, for an attorney to represent them at a real estate closing. Another example are the myriad attorneys lining the streets of the Bronx offering a divorce, from soup to nuts, for prices that even Crazy Eddie would declare to be "Insane".

attributed this at first to the stress and strain of the eviction proceeding. The proceeding was split between two justices of the local court. One justice had a reputation for being "dumb". This is not to say that the justice was unintelligent, although that could be said of a fair number of the currently sitting judges. In fact, "unintelligent" would be a compliment pertaining to some of the buffoons sitting on the bench. Rather, this judge is referred to as "dumb" because no one could ever hear a word he said from the bench. Those of you who have seen the old "Seinfeld" episode with Kramer's girlfriend, the "low talker" will know what I mean. The other Justice on the case was without a doubt the most senile member of the bench I have ever appeared before. This judge could only remember his name because of the nameplate sitting out on the bench in front of him. This justice has since done the legal community and the general public a great service by retiring. He is without a doubt in an assisted living community at this time, perhaps in the advanced stages of dementia.

Let's return to Mr. Johnson's story. Mr. Johnson's demise was the arrogant attitude of the tenant. This tenant was a fast learner. He quickly sized up the court and realized that he could play this matter out indefinitely without ever having to pay rent. We refer to these types as "Professional Tenants". As a result of filing the eviction case in this kangaroo court we went from a situation where the tenant was only slightly behind in his rent to a fiasco where the tenant was living rent-free for about 6 months. No matter what I did, I could not convince the court to give me a trial date. The court kept adjourning the case and directing the tenant over and over again to make payment of the rent. Nonetheless, the tenant never paid the rent. Each time, the court would again order the tenant to pay the rent by a date certain or else the court would issue an eviction warrant. However, each time we would come to court, the judge would simply re-issue the same order all over again. After about 3 or 4 examples of this type of nonsense, I began ordering the court stenographer's transcripts of these court appearances and showing the judge his own order in writing: All to no avail.

After about 6 or 7 months of this the court issued yet another "final" order to the tenants to pay up or get out, and it appeared that the court really was serious this time. I wasn't holding my breath. The judge ordered the tenants to pay all rent owed by June 29th, or to get out by June 30th.

An attorney never knows exactly what is going on in any given client's head at any given moment. My thought was that the tenant would neither pay the money nor get out of the house by the 30th of June. The only way to determine this is to check the house sometime on July 1st to see if the tenant is still there. If the tenant is still in residency, one must go through the process of having the local Constable or Sheriff pay a visit to the tenant and give the tenant what is essentially a 3 day notice to get out. If the tenant doesn't get out after the three days are up, the landlord must then have the Sheriff or Constable forcibly remove the tenant, as they used to say: "'Throw them out on the street.'". Things rarely, if ever, come to this pass.

As I said, this is what I was thinking. I had no idea what Mr. Johnson was thinking. I was soon to find out. Fortunately, I did not find out what Mr. Johnson was planning to do until after he had already done it. Equally fortunate (and well-planned) was the fact that my home telephone number was at that time, and remains to this day, unlisted. A word to the wise sole practitioner: keep your home telephone number to yourself! If you give it to your clients you deserve everything you get as a result.

Mr. Johnson had apparently taken the judge's "final" order very literally. He went to an all-night diner on June 29th and sat at a table drinking coffee while staring at the clock on the diner's wall until the very stroke of midnight. Midnight would then mean that June 29th had technically turned over to June 30th. He then got in his car and drove to the rental house. He arrived about ten minutes later. Mr. Johnson had a key to the house. He entered the front door and took notice that there was still furniture and personal belongings of the tenants within the living-room of the house. He nonetheless walked into the master bedroom, where, to his amazement (and you can imagine the tenants'), he found the tenant in bed with his wife. As you can imagine, from this point forward things got a bit out of hand. The tenant jumped up out of bed, threw on the light and seeing Mr. Johnson yelled something along the lines of "What the Hell are you doing here?" To which Mr. Johnson replied, "I was going to ask you the same thing!" Exit stage left. The next scene finds Mr. Johnson tumbling down a long flight of stone stairs leading from the front door of the house down to the street below. This after Mr. Johnson had taken several good punches to the head, courtesy of the tenant.

The next scene finds Mr. Johnson in the custody of the Sheriff's Department, handcuffed, and on his way to the local hospital and psychiatric center. To add insult to injury, Mr. Johnson is arraigned on charges of burglary, trespass and assault against the tenant. *The judge who is called in the middle of the night to handle the arraignment is—you guessed it—one of the very same judges who was responsible for the whole fiasco to begin with.* The judge conducted the arraignment at Mr. Johnson's bed-side at the psychiatric unit of the hospital. In the meanwhile, Mr. Johnson's wife was attempting to contact me (at 3:00 o'clock in the morning) in order to assist at the bed-side arraignment. As I said before, my home telephone number is unlisted. Ignorance sometimes is bliss.

So how and when did I first find out about what occurred that evening? Well, the next day dawned as normal as one would expect. I had no court appearances that day so I happened to be in my office in the morning doing the usual things, taking the usual ridiculous phone calls, and shuffling papers from one side of my desk to the other. Suddenly, I heard my secretary cry out in the other room: "Oh my God, you're never going to believe what's walking in the door. Quick, hide under your desk!" But, I was trapped. It was too late to get out of my office without being seen. Another word to the wise: all professionals should have an escape route or hatch for unwanted visitors, a back door or a trap door out of the office. I did not have such a door, and since hiding under the desk was too risky (how do you explain this one if you are caught?), I decided to face the terror walking in the door. It was Mr. Johnson accompanied by his wife.

Mr. Johnson looked a good deal like Lon Chaney, Jr. from the old "The Mummy" films. His entire face, neck and most of his torso were wrapped up with gauze. Only the eyes, which were like burning flames, were visible. For the better part of an hour I sat at my desk and heard the tale I have just related to you: and I didn't laugh—that is until Mr. Johnson left the office.

There is, of course, another method of securing the departure of an unwanted tenant from one's rental property. This is the "non-legal" ("self-help"), or shall we say "illegal" method, which this author cannot condone, although with what I know about landlord/tenant cases, I might be tempted to use this method if the situation involved one of my own tenants. Sometimes, this extra-judicial manner of eviction can be far less costly than the traditional court process. It can be much more expedient and a good deal less aggravating than plodding one's way through the landlord-tenant court process.

We now come to the case of our friendly neighborhood landlord, Mr. Cash. Mr. Cash owned a rental property in what can only be described as a run down, "you know you've hit rock bottom when you're living there" sort of area. Mr. Cash's tenant was an arrogant chap, who utterly refused to pay his rent, and told Mr. Cash flat out that he was a "professional tenant". He bragged that he knew just how to work the court system and he assured Mr. Cash that he would be "living rent-free" for many months if Mr. Cash attempted to evict him.

Well, I have to say that Mr. Cash showed some ingenuity. He and his son, a scary looking guy, who looked like he had just been released from the Riker's Island Jail in New York City, showed up at the rental property at the crack of dawn one morning. Using a saber saw, they sawed the hinges off the front door of the apartment. As you can imagine, the tenant could not help but hear the ensuing racket. After sawing off the hinges, Mr. Cash and his son lifted the door out of its frame and asked the tenant if he would like to leave. As you can imagine, the gust of wind rushing past Mr. Cash and his son was preceded by the tenant and whatever personal belongings he could quickly grab. They never heard from the tenant again. A very much illegal—yet highly successful eviction—and very cost effective too: they didn't even break the saw blade, although they did have to spend about $10.00 on new door hinges.

The bottom line: the solution to the landlord-tenant problem is really very simple. A landlord should not be saddled with a tenant who is either unable to afford to pay the rent or who simply wants a free ride. The legislature has to finally recognize the obvious fact that the procedures for obtaining a court eviction are too slow, costly and cumbersome. There is also too much discretion given to the local judges. A landlord, by owning a property and deciding to rent it out, does not thereby become a charitable organization responsible for the housing of persons who cannot afford to pay the rent. By the same token, a tenant, who pays the rent (or who stands ready, willing and able to pay the rent) should be entitled to a safe, clean, functional rental property. Toilets and sinks should work. A tenant should not be freezing to death in the winter or roasting in the summer.

Courts are funny creatures. They know damn well that both the tenant and the landlord are lying to some extent. The rental property cannot simultaneously be the Taj Mahal, as testified to by the landlord. Nor can it be cannery row, as testified to by the tenant. The truth must lie somewhere in between. The courts listen to testimony about the rental property *while the landlord, tenant and the judge are physically present in the courtroom.* The courts sometimes look at self-serving, often times doctored-up photographs of the property taken by each party to the dispute. *But nobody ever bothers to actually go to the property.* This isn't to suggest that judges have the time or the inclination to do so. However, neutral property inspectors, hired by the court with the parties to split the cost, would go a long way toward solving the "He said, She said" problem inherent in all landlord/tenant disputes. The court system uses neutral evaluators in other matters, such as child custody disputes, and neutral appraisers of property in matrimonial matters. My suggestion to the court system is: "Try it, you might like it".

Landlord-tenant cases are the fodder of good tales. A colleague recently handled an eviction matter against a tenant (who refused to pay rent) and her basement squatter. A squatter is essentially a person who moves into a place of abode without the permission or knowledge of the landlord. The tenant finally reluctantly agreed to move out. However, she was then persuaded by the squatter to fight it out with the landlord in court on the basis of the lack of "habitability" of the premises. This means that the tenant claimed that the premises lacked essential services, such as heat, hot water, and the like.

All seemed to be going well with this stalling tactic until on the first court appearance, the landlord first met the squatter and recognized him as a gentleman of Arabic descent who was on the FBI's Most-Wanted list. Exit the landlord from the court. Enter the FBI and Secret Service, and away went the squatter. This would be the fortuitous method of evicting squatters. The moral of the story for the landlord: sometimes the squatter not only does not belong in your property, he also does not belong in this country. The moral for the squatter: if the justice system is already looking for you it is probably not a good idea to show up voluntarily in court.

In another classic landlord-tenant dispute, I once represented a landlord seeking the eviction of a dry-cleaning establishment from a commercial building. No sooner did I file the eviction case, than the tenant obtained an attorney who filed not one, but two cases against my client seeking tens of millions of dollars in alleged damages for supposedly destroying the tenant's business. This is from a tenant which did not pay its rent for a year and a half. It took almost three years, including two trials, three courts and one appeals court to finally secure the eviction of this crack-pot tenant. Following the eviction, the Sheriff pad-locked the establishment, causing quite a local stir because the drycleaner/tenant was in possession of clothing belonging to many other cleaners, and, in turn, to many other people. Not a day went by that I did not receive telephone calls from irate customers demanding their shirts, skirts and suits: all of which were locked up in the dry-cleaning establishment.

Since the eviction, I have been advised of a mortgage foreclosure and real estate tax foreclosure on this gentleman's home. Apparently, this fine gentleman has failed to pay his mortgage for approximately three years, during which time he has continued to live well in the premises. At least he didn't discriminate against my client. Apparently, he never paid anybody.

In another residential case, I was once hired to evict a gentleman from a condominium in Westchester County, New York. This tenant was another professional tenant. This gentleman's modus operandi was to move into someone else's home, pay the first month's rent and then never pay another dime. Immediately upon moving in, he would start haranguing the landlord with telephone calls and certified letters regarding a host of alleged problems with the home, including lack of heat, water leaks and the like. He would make wild claims of damage to his furniture and personal belongings and the like. Then, he would refuse to permit the landlord entry to the premises to check on the supposed damage. On my way to court one day on an unrelated case, I saw this gentleman standing in front of me (I did not know who he was since we had never met). He was filing a summons and complaint against my clients for alleged damages to his personal property, furniture, clothing and the like. I could see the suit papers over his shoulder as I was idly waiting on line to file my own case. This was shortly after my clients had hired me to evict him. He beat us to the punch, so the landlord not only had to prosecute the eviction case in one court, but he also had to defend this stupid case brought by the crooked tenant in a different court. When all was said and done, I finally secured the eviction, and got the other ridiculous case dismissed, only to find out that the tenant had filed for bankruptcy: which gained him another three months in the condominium free of charge. The bankruptcy petition named at least thirty creditors, including numerous former landlords, and several hundred thousand dollars in unpaid debts. The last time I saw the tenant was a couple of years ago. He was behind the wheel of a brand new car with custom license plates. God help his current landlord!

This is a good time to introduce my Top 10 Reasons why lawyers don't like their clients:

1. clients don't pay their bills but even when they do, they rarely pay on time;

2. clients don't reimburse you for money you pay out on their behalf;

3. They lie to you or they tell you what they think you need to know (as opposed to the truth);

4. They call you on the phone constantly to tell you the same things over and over again—as if you didn't get it the first five times (clients like to refer to this as "touching base");

5. They show up at your office unannounced and expect you to drop everything you are doing and meet with them;

6. They make ridiculous (sometimes even fraudulent) demands and assume everything is an emergency even when it isn't;

7. They don't take the advice you give them;

8. They call you early in the morning and late in the evening, and at home, if you are stupid enough to give out your home telephone number[3];

9. They cause you surprise at trial by springing documents on you at the eleventh hour, when it is too late to do anything about it;

10. They do illegal things and then tell the whole World that you advised them to do it; and,

11. They don't pay their bills (Oh, I think we mentioned that one already).

My former client, Mr. Mayhem and his cohorts embodied in abundance each and every one of the top ten reasons why lawyers don't like their clients. Mr. Mayhem was engaged in a variety of businesses. He was a landlord, owning several buildings, each of which had a plethora of building code violations and fire code violations. When I served an eviction notice[4] on one of the tenants in a residential property owned by Mr. Mayhem, I could not help but notice the dirt floor of the apartment. The tenant, a young woman, showed up to the eviction proceeding with her newborn baby. This is a customary ruse in eviction proceedings and has often made me wonder whether the child actually belongs to the tenant or whether the tenant has simply borrowed the child from a friend or relative just for the occasion. In any event, on this one occasion it happened to be several days prior to Christmas: prompting the judge to ask me if I really believed that he would evict the tenant and her baby so close to Christmas. I didn't, and he didn't either.

Mr. Mayhem had a partner, Mr. Murder, who obtained loans for people who could not possibly have gotten loans on their own since these persons had questionable credit, insufficient income, bankruptcies and other financial and legal problems. Of course these loans came with a hefty price-tag, which was usually foisted upon the unsuspecting borrower at the closing table when there was really nothing the borrower could do about it. I recall one borrower, a security guard by trade, who believed that Mr. Murder would show up at the closing. For this reason, he had brought his gun to the closing. As you can imagine, I was somewhat

---

3. As a general rule, it is suicidal to give out one's home telephone number to a client, or to maintain a listed telephone number.

4. When one first starts out as a sole practitioner, he or she usually cannot even afford to hire a professional process server, so the attorney serves the suit papers. I used to do this at one time in order to save money, that is, until I was chased off a defendant's property by two pit-bull terriers. After that, I decided to leave this job to the professionals. I now use a process server, who is a retired police officer, as most are. He carries at least three guns on his person at any given time.

relieved to tell him that the broker would not be appearing at the closing.[5] I can't stand the sight of blood.[6]

As an aside, people generally despise mortgage brokers, sometimes even more so than attorneys. If you are a mortgage broker, by trade, you would be well advised not to appear at closings. Let the bank's attorney collect your check and mail it to you: you may have to wait for your money a few days longer but it is infinitely safer and far less aggravating than having to hear the borrower bitch and moan at closing about what a lousy deal you brokered for him or her, or worse, run the risk of being shot.

Our friend, Mr. Murder subsequently teamed up with a partner and started a restaurant business. The partners renovated a decrepit old restaurant; putting far more money into the building than the building itself was worth. The money was all "borrowed"[7], for lack of a better word, from the partners' respective families. Our heroes signed a long-term lease for the building, with a hefty rent. They couldn't lose, or so they thought. That was, until it occurred to them that some-where along the line revenue must eventually exceed expenses or you cannot stay in business. In this case, revenue never did. What ended up happening was that our heroes helped themselves to whatever money there was and nobody else got paid: not the landlord; not the companies who supplied food to the restaurant; not the tradespersons who re-built the restaurant; nobody. You name it, every-body was stiffed. And, naturally, the family members who lent our heroes the money never saw their money again.[8] I was left to pick up the pieces and navigate through the myriad lawsuits which followed this fiasco. The restaurant corpora-

---

5. Mr. Murder never showed up at any of the closings he had brokered. I wonder why not?

6. There is an old joke that a lawyer is a Jewish man who couldn't stand the sight of blood: implying, of course, that if he could stand the sight of blood he would have become a doctor. I think this statement is fairly accurate, except that it applies to all genders, races and creeds.

7. I'll never forget my first experience with "borrowing". I lent $50.00 to a chiseler in college so that he could rent a tuxedo for a concert recital. Needless to say, he never paid me back. He did, however, show me a beautiful, brand new bicycle he had just purchased for several hundred dollars, when I asked for my money back. I had always thought that implied in the act of borrowing was that the person doing the borrow-ing meant to pay back the lender.

8. The only people who saw any money were the meat and fish providers from the pack-ing districts, since these folk have different, shall we say, more creative ways of mak-ing people pay their bills.

tion was denuded of all its assets and permitted to die, in a manner somewhat akin to a mercy killing.

Then there was Mr. Schemer's greeting card business. Mr. Schemer determined to set up a greeting card business. He began by hiring a graphic artist to sketch a card to be used for Valentine's Day. He then hired a printing firm to print up the many cards anticipated to be sold. The advertising blitz then began, including appearances on live radio programs. Finally, persons were hired to facilitate the actual sales, including manning the telephones, taking the orders, placing cards in envelopes and, of course, delivering the cards. Well, Mr. Schemer sold an awful lot of cards. However, the artist never got paid. The printer never got paid. The delivery company never got paid. The advertising company never got paid. The radio station never got paid. Need I continue? In short, nobody received one dime from the transaction, with the exception of Mr. Schemer, who subsequently abandoned the company and split with the money: Another American success story.

Many persons have poor credit, and they will do anything to fix it. Simply put, the best way to repair one's credit is "Time" and "Money". If you pay your bills as and when you are supposed to, over time, your credit will be restored. It's really quite simple. But, in our society of quick fixes, for every problem there is offered a supposed solution. And for every supposed solution there is an enterprising crook waiting in the wings to cash in on the unsuspecting. Ms. Cleaner fell into the latter category. Ms. Cleaner set up a multi-state "Credit Cleaning" or "Credit Repair" company, which was supposed to use certain magical formulas to "clean" bad credit. Each state generally has laws regulating such businesses, including a blanket prohibition on these companies receiving up-front monies from clients to perform such work. In this instance, Ms. Cleaner managed to convince many (to put it politely) weak-minded individuals to part with thousands of dollars of their hard-earned money with the promise that Ms. Cleaner's company would restore their credit. Their bad credit would be cleaned and their perfect credit rating from many years prior would be restored. They could now obtain a loan just like anybody else. Needless to say, the only cleaning that occurred was that of the wallets of the people who sent Ms. Cleaner their money.

Then there is the tale of Mr. Snort. This gentleman came to the office of a colleague seeking representation on allegations that he was in possession of cocaine and for allegedly distributing cocaine. The attorney could see that this representation was going to be a great deal of work so he quoted the prospective client a substantial retainer. The client did not object to the amount of the retainer, but asked if he could possibly pay the attorney—in cocaine, rather than money.

In the State of New York, a tax is assessed against the seller of real estate, called the transfer tax. The transfer tax is based upon the gross sale price of the property. The transfer tax is payable to the State of New York. In addition to this, if there is a gain on the sale of real property, the Federal Government (and sometimes State Government), under certain circumstances, assesses a Capital Gains Tax. Both of these "taxes" are based upon the gross amount of money reported from the sale. A colleague represented a client who was selling commercial property. Towards the end of the closing, the client requested that he and the buyer be left alone to have a brief discussion about the deal. About five minutes later, the clients asked that the attorneys re-enter the room. All seemed well and the closing proceeded. Following the closing, the attorney entered the men's bathroom where he saw the client strapping a pistol to his side, and closing a briefcase filled with cash: So much for the transfer tax.

The Matrimonial Client: Simply put, any practicing attorney will tell you that there is nobody worse or zanier than the matrimonial client. This client, by definition, is completely unable to separate themselves from the issues of the lawsuit. The reason is simple. The matrimonial lawsuit involves virtually every aspect of a person's life: where he or she lives, with whom he or she lives; with whom he or she cannot live; whether one has children and is allowed to keep them or not; whether one has money and is allowed to keep it or not; and so on. *The matrimonial client is, therefore, understandably obsessed with the case.* This holds equally true for attorneys who quite often can find themselves in the position of the matrimonial client of some other attorney. No matter what way you slice it, each matrimonial client believes that his or her case is the most important case on your agenda, and believes that you should have no agenda other than to work on his or her case on a daily basis. Every matrimonial client wants you to be his or her own exclusive attorney. In other words, the matrimonial client wants you to toil on his or her case on a 24/7 basis, but believe me, the client has no intention of paying the attorney accordingly.

People involved in matrimonial actions fight over the strangest things. One of my favorites is the childless couple who did not own a home and had precious few assets between them. They disputed virtually everything, which, of course, amounted to a hill of beans. It took almost two years and a lot of arm-twisting to convince the respective clients to settle their case. However, most of the settlement discussions involved not whether and how much of the husband's business the wife would be entitled to, but instead which party was going to "get custody" of which dog, and what the "visitation" rights would be. The parties had two dogs, so one party suggested that each party receive a dog.[9] This sounded reasonable until the other party refused, claiming that the dogs considered themselves to be "siblings" and could not possibly be separated from each other. This is the "All or Nothing" approach to settlement. When this seemingly impossible item was finally worked out and the settlement papers were ready to be signed, the wife refused to sign the agreements. It had just occurred to her that when the dogs died she would like to have them cremated and keep their remains. The "remains" of the to-be-cremated dogs (note that these dogs were alive, young and well at the time) almost ruined the settlement of the entire case. "Ashes to ashes, fun to funky, we know Major Tom's a junky ..."

The "Here's Johnny" Matrimonial Client: When an attorney shows up at the office early, this can mean only one thing: the attorney is behind on paperwork and is attempting to catch up. Most attorneys know that the bulk of the paperwork required in a law practice must be done before the hour of 9:00 am or after 5:00 pm when the telephone ceases to ring, or at least slows down. The typical 9:00 am to 5:00 pm day is spent jumping from one phone line to the next. So if your lawyer happens to be at her desk at 7:30 in the morning, you can rest assured that this is her catch-up time. One fine morning, I appeared at the office bright and early (around 7:00 am) to play a little catch-up ball. No sooner did I plant my buttocks upon the seat than the telephone rang. The first call from Mrs. Phillips was to the effect that she feared her husband would be coming over to her apartment (they were no longer residing together) to demand that she hand over the children. The second call from Mrs. Phillips, which came about fifteen minutes later, stated her concern that her husband was on his way over to the apartment. The third call from our client indicated that the husband had entered the driveway area in front of the apartment. The fourth call was interrupted by a loud, banging sound and the wife frantically screaming to me that her husband was chopping his way through the front door with an axe. This turned out to be true. Fortunately the husband's chop was worse than his bite: having chopped down the front door, he then quietly left. Shelley Duvall, in "The Shining", wasn't so fortunate. Needless to say, I did not catch-up on anything that morning. "Here's Johnny!"

One of my all-time favorite matrimonial clients would have to be Mr. Brown. Mr. Brown reminded me of Alec Baldwin's character in the film "Married to the Mob". For anyone who has not seen the film, Baldwin plays a small-time hood in a Mafia family. He is married to a bimbo played by Michelle Pfeiffer. Pfeiffer's

---

9.   This would seem far preferable to the approach of wise King Solomon, whereby each party might receive one half of each dog.

character, fed up with the marriage, finally blurts out in a thick Brooklyn twang to Baldwin's character: "I want a divorce!" to which the character portrayed by Baldwin replies: "You can't have one." Mr. Brown simply refused for almost five years, to let his wife have a divorce. Quite possibly, love had very little to do with the refusal. Mr. Brown knew full well that no divorce meant that there would be no property settlement. No property settlement meant that he maintained effective control over all of the parties' properties because his wife had become so miserable living with Mr. Brown that she had moved out of the house; taking nothing with her but the clothes on her back. In short, she lived throughout the pendency of the case[10] in poverty. And, the case lasted a long time. After about five years of fighting; trial; appeals; and countless court appearances, Mr. Brown begrudgingly agreed to settle the case. Somehow Mrs. Brown's personal jewelry, clothes, and effects never did make it back to her. There was a rumor circulating to the effect that these items were sealed into the trunk of an automobile, the whereabouts of which no one seemed to know. Mr. Brown always took the position that he had no idea where these items were. I suppose we will never know.

Some clients are quick to file suit but they don't really want to go to trial. People outside the legal profession assume that when a person files suit, the complaining party lives for his or her "Day in Court". This is usually a fallacy. What the complaining party wants is usually money—not a day in court, because a day in court guarantees nothing. A quick settlement in which the client obtains his or her objectives, or at least most of them, is really what most rational clients desire. A colleague had the misfortune to represent a woman in a personal injury case, having been retained for the specific purpose of trying the case. There is an old adage that one cannot serve two masters: he will hate the one and obey the other. Maybe he will hate both. Or, maybe he will try to reconcile both masters even though they have divergent goals. The latter is what happened to the attorney in this case.

The client desperately wanted to settle the case because she said that she could not endure a trial. The attorney who delegated the case to the trial lawyer for trial, refused to permit the client to settle the case. Now, of course, this is impermissible. If a client wants to settle a case, no matter how ridiculous the attorney thinks the settlement is, he must effectuate the client's wishes. In this instance, the other attorney convinced the client, against her better judgment, that the case had to be tried and that no settlement should be accepted. Despite having a rea-

---

10. When lawyers say "pendency of the case", they refer to the amount of time it takes the case to go to trial or settle from the time it is first filed with the court.

sonable offer on the table from the defendant, the offer was rejected and the case proceeded to trial. In the midst of the client's testimony, she began hyperventilating to the point where paramedics had to be rushed into the courtroom: taking the client out on a stretcher with oxygen mask affixed. As one would imagine this scene resulted in a mistrial: meaning that the case had to be tried all over again before a different jury. The most astounding part of the story is that the defendant maintained its reasonable offer, and the other attorney still refused to permit his client to accept the settlement. Needless to say, the trial attorney did not try the case the second time around. Fool me once, shame on you. Fool me twice, shame on me.

In much the same category as the above is the client who does not wish to go to trial, and who does not wish to settle, but wants the money nonetheless. A colleague recently handled a case where the client, a young imposing sort of gentleman, was giving testimony at trial in support of his case. During the course of the testimony, the client insisted on blurting out things that the judge had ruled were inadmissible. After several strongly-worded cautions from the judge, the client left the courthouse during the lunch break, never to return. At the close of the lunch recess, the attorney asked the stepfather of the plaintiff where his son was, to which the stepfather replied, "I gave him cab fare and sent him home". Naturally, the attorney called his client and told him that a witness cannot simply leave the witness stand in the midst of testifying. The client told the attorney, "I am done with this fucking case. Settle it." Miraculously, the attorney was able to effectuate a settlement in his client's absence.

Following the settlement, the attorney prepared the usual settlement papers, including what is known as a "General Release"[11]. For the general release to be effective, it must be signed by the client. Several weeks went by and the attorney still did not have the release signed by the client. The attorney called the client and wrote several letters to the client in an effort to obtain the release. Finally, the client called the attorney and told him that he refused to sign the release. The attorney told the client that he could not conclude the settlement without the release and he could not obtain the settlement monies. Time went by, and the attorney did not hear from the client. Out of the blue, the client materialized at the attorney's office demanding "the money". When the attorney told the client (for the fourteenth time) that he had no money because the client had refused to

---

11.   A General Release or General Release of Liability states that the party doing the releasing will never again sue or make a claim against the party being released based upon anything that happened to the date of the Release.

sign the release, the client picked up all the files on the attorney's desk and threw them in his face. He then hurled a lamp at the attorney. The attorney managed to block this toss. Then the client charged the attorney and started swinging. The client's mother stepped in between. The attorney's secretary called the police, who arrived and chased the client out of the office and down the street where they arrested him on assault charges.

The Word of God Client. I once represented a woman in connection with a personal injury claim involving a slip and fall in a supermarket. These cases are more difficult for claimants to win than people generally think. Most people think that the mere act of falling is sufficient to sustain the lawsuit. Not so. The claimant's attorney must prove that the defendant (in this case the store where the woman fell) had "actual" or "constructive knowledge" of the dangerous condition for a reasonable time prior to the accident, so that the defendant had the opportunity to remedy the condition. Of course, no defendant is going to admit that it knew of a dangerous condition but decided not to do anything about it. In this situation, one must prove that the condition existed for such a period of time that the defendant should have known about it, and had a "reasonable" period of time to remedy it. Our case was very tough because all the facts indicated that the dangerous condition had occurred just immediately prior to the client's fall. This would result in a dismissal of the case. Somehow, miraculously, I was able to develop a rapport with the insurance claims adjuster and—I think because we got along so well—he offered $25,000 to settle the case. I thought I had the client most of the way toward accepting this generous offer, when the client called me one day to tell me that I was "fired". It seems that God had told her in the middle of the night that she should not accept the settlement. She then went to another law firm, which, after a protracted litigation, ended up settling the case for the same $25,000. I suppose God isn't as infallible as we were led to believe.

In a similar case handled by a colleague, the Plaintiff was ever so slightly injured in an automobile accident in New York. Most people believe the mere fact that an accident occurs and it is the other driver's fault is the claimant's ticket to wealth. Not so. Most states have what are referred to as "No-Fault" or "Threshold" statutes which essentially eliminate the right to sue a negligent driver for pain and suffering and all non-out of pocket loss unless a particular type of injury is sustained. New York State has perhaps the harshest no-fault law in the nation.[12] In any event, this client clearly did not have damages even approaching the seriousness of injuries required to meet the no-fault threshold. Nonetheless, my colleague proceeded with the case (probably because he had just started his own practice and would take any client who walked in the door). On the day of trial the trial judge held a conference in which he attempted to settle the case.[13] The judge miraculously obtained the agreement of the insurance defense attorneys to pay a good sum of money to the claimant to dispose of the claim. However, the client, who could be seen on his knees praying in the courthouse men's room, refused all offers of settlement. Apparently, God and his angels had told the client that the jury would vindicate him and that he should accept no settlement. Amazingly, as each day of the trial unfurled and the testimony started to mount against the claimant, the trial judge continued to push the parties toward settlement. The trial judge managed to convince the defense firm to maintain its fair settlement offer throughout the trial, even though it had become fairly obvious that the jury was going to dismiss the case from about the second day of trial. The trial lasted two full weeks. The claimant continued to pray in the courthouse men's room and continued to refuse his counsel's advice to take the settlement, or else run a very serious risk of having his case thrown out by the jury. After the jury has deliberated and come to a decision (what we attorneys call a "Verdict"), there is a brief period where the attorneys (who have been sitting around doing nothing waiting for the jury to make its decision) must straighten themselves and their respective clients up and await the jury's return to the courtroom. At this point, however, the claimant was nowhere to be found. His counsel, after being given the appropriate threats from the judge, ran out into the courthouse hallways in an attempt to find the client. He found him, as you would guess, on his

---

12. New York Insurance Law Article 51 says essentially that even if the other driver was entirely at fault, and you were badly hurt, you cannot sue for your pain and suffering unless you either have economic losses (such as loss of income and medical expense) in excess of $50,000.00, or you have sustained what the statute describes as a "serious injury". Even though the statute hasn't changed in a long, long time, the courts in New York seem to be finding that fewer and fewer injuries are "serious" enough to meet the threshold. This has developed an entire cottage industry of so-called "threshold motions", wherein the insurance defense attorneys will routinely file a motion to dismiss prior to the trial of any personal injury case arising out of an automobile accident, regardless of the injuries sustained, claiming that the no-fault "threshold" has not been met by the claimant. These firms figure they have nothing to lose. They are usually right. Up until fairly recently, claimants' attorneys had just assumed that a herniated lumbar, thoracic or cervical disc, demonstrated by an MRI (Magnetic Resonance Imaging Scan) was in and of itself sufficient to meet the threshold. Any orthopedist or neurologist will tell you that this is indeed a serious injury to the spine. However, the New York courts, in their infinite wisdom, have now taken the position that to meet the no-fault threshold, "you've got to show us more" than a "mere" herniated disc.

knees in the men's room praying for his verdict. He had to be dragged into the courtroom to hear the verdict. His prayers were not answered. The jury dismissed his case, as well it should have. The moral of the story is that if you have hired an attorney and the attorney has a fair level of experience, and the attorney and judge both agree as to a particular dollar value for a settlement: take the money. Don't go consulting God. God really doesn't care about jury verdicts. There are plenty of other, more important issues on God's plate.

In the "I'm tired of taking this crap from clients" category: is the situation a colleague found herself in. The clients were two elderly persons who came to the office for preparation of a will and other estate planning. After the clients left the office, the attorney noticed a rather distinct odor: the office smelled like a men's room after a hockey game. To put it as bluntly as possible, the clients, who were incontinent, crapped in the reception area of the attorney's office.

To drink or not to drink, that is the question: I once met with a couple of pro-spective clients, who insisted on meeting at a local diner. These people were apparently under the impression that we could sit in this diner for whatever amount of time we wanted, and use a table without purchasing anything to eat. A few trips to the table by the glaring waiter finally succeeded in convincing them otherwise. At 11 o'clock in the morning, the gentleman client ordered a glass of wine. After being harangued (rightfully so) by his wife about drinking wine in the morning, the prospective client went to take the first sip. But, he never made it. Instead, he threw the entire glass of wine all over me, drenching me and my note-pad from head to toe. I sat there staring at these bizarre people, with wine drip-ping into the pockets of my suit jacket and into my shoes. Needless to say, I excused myself as gracefully as I could and the prospective clients never heard from me again. This was one instance where I felt entirely justified in not return-ing a potential client's telephone calls.

Not to be outdone on the drinking scene, I once represented a client in con-nection with a driving while intoxicated charge.[14] I met with the client in an

---

13.   I don't know why fewer and fewer judges will now invest a little time in attempting to settle a case. I have had many cases settle as a result of the trial judge's active "push-ing" of the respective clients and attorneys toward a fair resolution of the dispute. Sometimes a mule needs a good push for its own sake. Good judges will spend the time, often with the result that a trial will be unnecessary, and far less burdensome to the judiciary system. Settlements are also a good thing for people who are potential jurors: dragged out of their jobs and lives to sit on a case for God only knows what length of time, simply because one side or the other, or both, can't sit down like rea-sonable persons and reach a settlement.

attempt to get a feeling for just how much the client had to drink on the night in question, how much he had to eat, how far apart the eating, drinking and driving were, and the like. I ran out of paper, jotting down the number and type of drinks. Mind you, this was a typical weeknight. In the client's mind, it was not out of the ordinary to put away six to eight beers, a glass or two of wine and a couple of whisky's in a two hour period. On the day of the first court appearance, I was arguing to the judge that the client should receive the conditional driving permit, which would have permitted him to drive back and forth to work during the pendency of the case. The argument was going well, until someone tapped me on the shoulder and asked me if I was paying much attention to my client. Actually, I was so focused on the judge and the prosecutor, that I had paid very little attention to my client, who, as it turns out, was very obviously stoned drunk for the court appearance. It probably states the obvious, but if one is brought before the court on a DWI or DUI charge, it is probably not a very good idea to show up to court inebriated. Surely, if one is brought to court on charges of theft, you wouldn't expect the defendant to try to pick a juror's pocket during the trial. But, perhaps we attorneys should guard ourselves better against the obvious. In any event, somehow the judge failed to notice my client's horrendous condition, and granted him the conditional driving license. Fortunately, no one died as a result of my client remaining on the road as a driver: at least not while I represented him.

A colleague once took a significant Japanese client to Yankee Stadium for a ball game. In the middle of the game, a fine patron seated in the upper deck decided to pour a large beer over the railing, which, of course, landed directly on the client's head, drenching him. This put, shall we say, a "damper" on the relationship between the attorney and the client.

In the "Who's the client anyway?" category: I once handled a mortgage foreclosure for a bank involving a commercial property in Connecticut. The foreclosure involved a dispute amongst quite a few banks, which had all lent substantial money to the same deadbeat and gotten burned. The banks were jockeying for position to see who would get paid first from the limited proceeds of the foreclosure sale. My client (Bank A) found itself in a position where if it won priority, it would virtually eliminate the ability of Bank B to recover any real money. Naturally, I did everything within my power to make sure that Bank A defeated Bank

---

14.   The term "drunk driving" is rarely, if ever, found in the penal codes of the 50 states. It is usually referred to either as "driving while intoxicated" or "DWI" or "driving under the influence" or "DUI".

B. The only problem was that toward the end of the case, Bank B was taken over by Bank C. And, Bank C, whom I so nicely defeated, turned out, unbeknownst to me, to be a major client of the firm I was employed by. In short, I had managed to defeat my own client.

I once represented a client who seemed to walk around with a dark cloud over his head. We will refer to him as John. John purchased a condominium in New York which was part of a development built by a plumber-turned developer. Shortly after the purchase, John married Dusk and they headed back home to their new unit. As John carried his bride across the threshold he noticed something not just right in the living-room. Apparently, the next door neighbor had thrown a party and one of the male guests, having consumed more than sufficient quantities of alcohol to lose all inhibitions, waltzed into the wrong unit (John's unit), stripped down naked and passed out on the sofa. This fine gentleman awoke to the sounds of Dusk's screams and the dull thump of John's foot striking his buttocks as John alternately chased and kicked him a mile down the road. The villain attempted escape into the woods, where he was apprehended shortly thereafter by the local police, with the aid of police dogs. Hiding in the woods, naked, beaten and freezing from the cold was a bit more than he could stand.

Not long after this incident, John and Dusk started to notice unusual things about their brand new condominium unit. There was a constant leak in a skylight in the upstairs bathroom, which always leaked into a bathtub positioned fortuitously beneath the skylight. Another strange thing occurred with the electric power. Lights would flicker and turn on and off by themselves. Appliances would shut off by themselves. The happy homeowners hired an electrician who decided to check out the basement. What he found in the brand new unit was large rats living in the walls and basement of the home, chewing through the power cables. A further inspection of the unit indicated that the problems John and Dusk did notice were insubstantial in comparison to the hidden construction errors lurking within the four walls of the unit. In the interim, the plumber/builder had filed for bankruptcy and the condominium development had been placed into a receivership. John and Dusk wisely decided to sell, and I was once again hired for the purpose of conducting the sale.

The first prospective purchaser John and Dusk had for the condominium unit from Hell, could not, at the last minute, qualify for a mortgage; therefore the first closing was aborted. John and Dusk began their search for another purchaser. The next purchaser obtained a mortgage, but mortgages must be loaned from a bank, and a bank must indeed exist. Well, the purchaser's bank existed: that is, until the night before the closing. In the wee hours of the morning prior to the closing an earthquake in California destroyed the purchaser's bank, sending John and Dusk once again back to square one.

The next time John and Dusk attempted to sell the unit, the closing was set and the bank had re-built from the earthquake. This time, in the middle of the evening prior to the morning closing, the pipes in the kitchen burst, tearing all the kitchen cabinets off the walls and cascading water through the sheetrock walls. John woke a good friend up in the middle of the night and they spent the entire evening putting the kitchen back together. The closing finally went forward and the paint was still drying when the new owner moved in.

John and Dusk's troubles had not yet ended. They had contracted to purchase a new single-family residence in a quiet neighborhood and the construction was completed just in time for them to move in. Naturally, I was called upon to handle this closing as well. The house seemed to be a dream home, that is, until about five years later when John and Dusk attempted to install a swimming pool. Have you ever wondered what your contractor does with all the garbage, refuse, bottles, cans, cigarette packs, twisted nails, broken sheetrock and incorrectly cut wood, pizza boxes and other trash, generated during the construction of a new home? Well, John and Dusk found out when they attempted to excavate their new swimming pool. Needless to say, the pool ended up costing them twice as much as the initial estimate, since the new excavator had to remove and cart away tons of garbage and junk buried in the backyard of the home by the original builder.

The Rich Client: Every lawyer wants to represent the "Rich" client. However, once you do land such a client you soon realize why the client is rich. I can assure you that the client did not become wealthy by paying substantial fees to his attorney. Rich clients usually turn out to be nothing but impossible, pushy, demanding cheapskates. Despite their unwillingness and slowness to pay their attorney, they will treat their attorney as though they were the attorney's only client. These clients challenge even the most reasonable legal bills: this is so, even after the attorney has virtually shut down his practice just to service the client.

I once represented a husband and wife team of real estate sharks. This couple's penchant was for finding poorly priced and depressed properties. They would buy them, fix them up for very little money (since they paid their contractors as poorly as they paid everyone else) and then they would scalp someone on the eventual sale. Every closing was a fiasco, as this couple would fight with everyone at the closing table over pennies. At one such closing, they had a particularly memorable dispute with a local real estate broker (who is also known in the community as a shark, of sorts), at which point the broker's son cursed me out and then picked up a handful of documents and threw them in my face.

At the time, my natural reaction was to beat the living daylights out of this brat. However, my thoughts went immediately to the New York State Grievance Committee, and I thought better—or worse—of it. The bottom line is that a real estate broker is permitted to curse out an attorney and even throw things in the attorney's face, and the broker won't lose his license. Should the attorney retaliate, however, the attorney can kiss his license to practice law goodbye.

The Arrogant Client: I once represented a client from Iran who was without a doubt the most arrogant client who has ever darkened my door. This client was a physician, and she never let a moment go by to lecture me on how much smarter she was than I; how worthless attorneys were to society; and, how fortunate I was to have her as a client. This client sought to sell "her" home in Chappaqua, New York[15]. However, after the title report[16] for the property arrived, it was fairly obvious that this woman did not actually own the home she was attempting to sell. Her husband did. Title was in his name alone. Thus, the wife, my client, had no authority whatsoever to pass title to the property. She could not sign the contract of sale as the seller, nor could she sign the deed over to the purchasers.

When I asked the client if I could meet with her husband to gain a power of attorney[17] or some other device to clear this matter up, she brushed my suggestion off as ridiculous, and told me that her husband was "unavailable". As it turned out, her husband was some do-gooder working for an organization in Cambodia: of all God-forsaken places. This put me in the unenviable position of having to get into contact with the husband in a country (if one can call it that) where the time zone makes it such that at no point in a waking day in Cambodia is it not an ungodly hour in the United States. I recall actually getting this gentleman on the telephone at about 1 o'clock in the morning (Eastern Standard Time) and speaking to him with gunfire blazing in the background. I then had to deal

---

15. Yes, this is the current home town of the famous Clinton family, or at least the home of former President William Jefferson Clinton.

16. A title report is the end-result of a search (usually conducted by what is referred to as a "title company" or "abstract company") of the status of title to a particular piece of real estate. The title or abstract company report provides the name or names of the current owners of the property, and any liens on the property, such as mortgages, judgments, tax liens and the like.

17. In this instance, a written direction, signed by the husband before a notary public giving the wife the ability (or power) to act in his behalf, to sign the contract of sale and to sign over the deed to the property.

with the United States Embassy in Cambodia, and I was finally able to obtain a power of attorney with which to close the transaction.

The closing itself was great sport as my client chiseled the last penny out of the poor buyer's pocket, to the point where I felt sorry for both the buyer and his hapless, not particularly experienced attorney. All throughout the closing, my client did not miss one opportunity to ridicule me, the bank's attorney, the buyer's attorney, the real estate broker and anyone else who had the misfortune to enter the room.

The only saving grace about such a closing is that the attorney gets paid at the closing and then can walk away, get into his car and hopefully never see the client again. However, in this instance it was not the case, thereby invoking a word to the wise: *never go to a closing or a trial, or anywhere else for that matter, in the same car as your client.* Following the event of the day, there will always be a reason for you to want to skip out on the client—win, lose or draw. In this instance, I had driven the client to the closing in my car. However, the closing was only about 15 miles from where I had picked the client up. Of course, on the way back from the closing—when I would have done anything to get away from this woman—I got stuck in a bumper-to-bumper traffic jam, which turned a twenty minute drive into an hour and a half nightmare. It was yet another ninety minutes that I had to endure this woman's scorn and ridicule. With any luck, she emigrated back to her native land and was eradicated in the long-term war between Iran and Iraq, which had been going on at the time.

The Sexy Client: The desire to represent the sexy client may be more a "male thing" than anything else, but I really can't say, having never been a woman. I once represented a nineteen year old client on a driving while intoxicated charge. I don't believe I actually met the woman before her court appearance date. I specifically advised the young woman to wear something "conservative" to court. I suppose I should have been more specific. The client indeed showed up to court in an outfit she apparently considered to be "conservative".[18] This young woman was gifted by God with a body somewhat akin to that of Monica Bellucci or Rebecca Romijn. The case was pending in one of the smaller courts in New York, what we refer to as the "Justice Courts". Some of these justice courts in the smaller towns and villages are little more than a small meeting room, with a seating capacity of less than 75 persons. When I entered the courtroom I couldn't help but notice my client sitting smack in the middle of the room wearing a hal-

---

18. If the outfit she wore to this court was "conservative", I shudder to think what she would consider "flashy", or "revealing".

ter top that barely covered her front, was completely open in the back—down to the small of her back—and what could have passed for painted-on shorts. Needless to say, the entire courtroom, including the judge (who was well into his 80's) was staring at my client.

I had a similar situation with a mother—daughter combination I once represented in connection with a personal injury claim. We were required to obtain the court's approval of the settlement for the fifteen year old daughter, and I was to drive the clients to the courthouse in the Bronx to meet with the presiding judge. My clients showed up at my office looking like the Judds: you couldn't tell which one was dressed in a more provocative manner, the mother or the daughter. It was a hot summer day and the clients had apparently dressed (if you can call it that) accordingly. Each was wearing what could have passed for painted-on mini-shorts, and a very revealing halter top. It was too late to send them home to re-dress, so I had to take them to court as they were.[19] The actual court appearance went well, as the judge appeared to fancy himself somewhat of a ladies' man. However, the nearest parking space I could get to the courthouse was over three city blocks away. I had to walk with these two women through endless cat-calls, like "Yo bitch"; "Yo, I got something for you right here, bitch"; "Yo, mama"; and, worse. It was just another day in court.

The Let's make a Mountain out of a Molehill Client: I once took to trial five parking tickets on behalf of a client. The trial lasted more than three hours, and I believe it may be the longest parking ticket trial in the history of New York jurisprudence. This woman had the misfortune of getting herself on the bad side of an overly-zealous local police officer. The officer issued five tickets. The concept behind one ticket was that my client's license plate was somehow "unreadable". This ticket had to be dropped during the trial because the officer could not offer any testimony as to why he felt this way (basically he made the charge up). Another charge was to the effect that my client's inspection sticker was not properly "affixed" to her windshield. In New York State, a motor vehicle must be inspected on a periodic basis, and a paper sticker is stuck onto the inside of the windshield to prove that the car indeed has passed the inspection. As a result of direct sunlight, magnified by the windshield, heat, cold and the like, these stickers invariably begin peeling away from the windshield not long after they are affixed. This is what happened to my client's sticker. One edge of the sticker was ever so slightly peeled away from the windshield, hence the ticket she received.

---

19. Okay, so this might be one exception to the "Don't ever drive in the same car as your client" rule.

Two other tickets involved my client's car supposedly being parked too far from the curb of the street. The problem with the one ticket was that there was no curb, and so the officer testified. The problem with the other ticket was that the officer issued the ticket following a huge snowstorm, where the officer actually got down and dug through approximately a foot of snow to even find the curb he claimed my client had parked too far away from[20]. The final ticket was issued with the claim that my client's car was parked within fifteen feet of a fire hydrant. There was only one major problem with this ticket. My client's car was on the opposite side of the street as the fire hydrant. Never, in my years of practice, have I even heard of such a charge. Nor had the judge. My client, who was always one step ahead of the police, set up a twenty-four hour a day, seven day per week surveillance camera, which caught this keystone cop using a tape measure to reach across the street to my client's car. Furthermore, he did this after my client had driven by in her other car, and had spoken with the cop asking him if anything was wrong with the way she had parked. The cop told her there was nothing wrong, but then when my client's moving car was out of sight, he took out his tape measure. This too was caught on the video.

The trial was a three-ring circus. The officer who issues the ticket usually presents his case to the court—on the rare occasions when anyone actually challenges these parking tickets. Here, a formal prosecutor was called in to try the case. This gentleman must have made at least fifty pointless objections during the course of the three hour trial. Furthermore, the local policemen's benevolent association sent yet another lawyer to "protect the interest" of the police officer who issued the ticket. I got home from this affair at about 1 o'clock in the morning. To add insult to injury, I struck a deer on the way home and wrecked my car: right around the corner from my home.

The Lucky Client: I once represented a client who was a livery cab driver defending against a speeding ticket. If the client was convicted of the ticket, he would clearly lose his driver's license, and his only chance of earning a living. In fact, there was very little the court or the arresting officer could do to help this gentleman, even if they were so inclined. The person's driving record was very poor.[21] I showed up for trial with my client, in the hope that the arresting officer would perhaps forget about the court date and fail to appear. In this way, the case would be dismissed for what is referred to as "failure to prosecute". Naturally in this instance, I was told that this particular police officer always showed up for

---

20.   I believe very strongly in the general integrity of our police, but this particular cop obviously needed to get a life.

court. But he didn't show up on this occasion. The arresting officer—a gentleman in his 50's—was himself arrested and indicted shortly before our traffic trial on charges of child molestation. Following his indictment, he killed himself with his own pistol. And, with this unfortunate officer, died the charges against my client.

The Not-So-Lucky Client, but The Lucky Attorney: A colleague once represented a client at a trial, where he desperately needed an adjournment to continue his preparation of the case. His adversary was not in an agreeable mood, and the court refused to grant the adjournment. The trial therefore began, with the attorney sweating it out wondering how he would be able to get a particular witness to court that he needed; how he would marshal his documents; how he would prepare his client adequately; and, how he would keep from having a nervous breakdown. As luck would have it, at the very outset of the trial, as the attorney called his client to the witness stand, the client walked to the front of the courtroom, tripped on a loose tile on the floor and landed headfirst into the bench, where she split her scalp open and had to be taken to the nearest hospital by ambulance. Thus, the attorney obtained a rather unusual adjournment of the trial. This is somewhat akin to taking one of Roger Clemens' fastballs on the buttocks just to get a man on first base.

The Two Minute IME Client: I once represented a woman who had several herniated discs arising out of an automobile accident. The defendant in the case availed itself—as defendants usually do—of an Independent Medical Examination, referred to as an "IME" in New York practice. An *Independent* Medical Examination is anything but "independent". The physicians who handle these examinations are usually the bottom feeders of their profession. They make a living by giving cursory examinations of claimants and then writing up the very same report (or slight variation thereof) for each and every claimant they examine. I could write these reports myself. Each report generally states that the claimant "appeared to be in no distress"; the claimant "made subjective complaints of discomfort", "the claimant's injuries, if any, have no causal relation to the acci-

---

21. Believe it or not, if one goes to court to defend against a traffic ticket, the arresting officer (or some other public official acting on the officer's behalf) will almost always agree to accept a guilty plea to a reduced charge. That is the end of the case, and there is no trial. Only a very small percentage of these cases actually go to trial. The prosecution in these cases relies heavily on the past driving record of the defendant in deciding whether and to what extent a plea deal will be crafted. In our instance, the client's driving record was so poor that there was little that could be done for him in the way of a deal.

dent, but pre-existed the accident", "the patient's complaints and injuries are resolved from the accident", and the like. No matter what the injury, the IME physician will say there is no injury, but even if there is an injury, the injury did not occur as a result of the accident the claimant is suing about. Something else caused the injury. And, in any event, the claimant is exaggerating the whole thing anyway.

On this particular occasion, this one purported physician examined my client by having her get up on a table, and then he looked at her for approximately five seconds. He never placed one hand on her or asked her to do anything. He didn't even check for a patella tendon reflex. When I handed this purported physician my client's X-Rays and MRI films showing the severe herniations to the discs of her cervical spine, he smiled and then handed them right back to me. He never took them out of their envelope.

He proceeded to write a report about one week later wherein he stated that my client had no injury whatsoever. This, despite the fact that my client had already undergone surgery to her spine, and at least two other physicians, who actually did examine the woman and read the X-Rays and MRI films (three physicians, if you count the radiologist); all found the same injuries. Again, we are not talking about the physician opining that my client's motor vehicle accident did not cause the injuries. We have a physician who did not conduct any examination or read the films. Yet, he testified that he did do so, and that he could find absolutely no injury. The curious part of the story is that I subsequently took my client to yet another physician hired by the same insurance carrier. This physician took me into his office and told me privately that the prior physician was essentially a liar and a crook because there was no way any doctor could have examined this woman, read the films, and not seen the obvious injuries to her spine. The bottom line: most IME physicians working for insurance carriers are crooks and liars: but not all. There are some with a higher degree of integrity. Unfortunately, these are few and far between.

The Forty-Five Minute IME Client: At the opposite end of the spectrum was the 20-something year old, very sexy female client with whom I attended an independent medical examination pertaining to a shoulder injury. The IME physician (a young male orthopedist) did everything he could to keep my client hanging around his office as long as possible. The examination took far longer than it should have taken for a shoulder injury, and curiously, involved the physician examining pretty much every area of this young woman's body. He even had her "dress", so to speak, in one of those hospital type gowns, which, if you have ever worn one, is essentially like wearing nothing at all. For her shoulder injury, she had her lower back, abdomen and legs examined over a lengthy period of time. This same client was actually propositioned for a date by the male anesthesiologist during her shoulder surgery, while the doctor was administering the anesthesia. Can you imagine, you, as a woman, being naked from the waste up, being drugged into a coma-like state, and your anesthesiologist is asking you out on a date? It kind of makes you wonder how the surgery went, doesn't it?

The Cheap Client: Without a doubt the most miserly client I have ever represented was a gentleman named Neil. Neil lived in a house which closely resembled the Munster's residence at 1313 Mockingbird Lane. Neil's presence was always preceded by the distinct odor of a person who never bathed or showered. In short, Neil stank. In fact, Neil bathed roughly once a week due to the fact that he was too cheap to spend money on hot water. Neil's home had a septic system, and those of us who have such systems (as opposed to municipal sewers), know that such systems must be pumped periodically. Since Neil didn't want to spend the money on a pumping service, he would urinate in a bucket during the week and then pour the contents of the bucket out into the public street. Neil drove a 40 year old car, which was literally dropping pieces of itself on the road as he would cruise by. You could hear Neil's car coming from a mile away. When I asked him why he didn't get a replacement muffler for his car, he told me that he had contacted General Motors, who advised him that GM no longer carried mufflers for a car this ancient.

Neil's wardrobe (unchanged in many years) looked somewhat like the old costumes worn by the 1980's progressive rock band Devo. He had everything but the saucer on his head. The only difference was that the Devo outfits were clean: Neil's were as filthy as he was. His wardrobe was rivaled only by that of his sister: a bearded three hundred fifty pound woman who once tried to convince a friend to "borrow" gowns from the local hospital[22] so that she could make dresses out of them.

When Neil was younger and had a wife and children, he used to walk the family down the street to his father's home every night for dinner. He didn't want to spend money on groceries. He kept all the lights off in the house to save on electricity. In later years (after the eventual divorce), he hooked up with a poor, unsuspecting woman who was particularly down on her luck. She moved in to the house of horrors. He charged her for electricity, the telephone bill and the food she ate.

---

22. The same type of gown the sexy IME client was made to wear for her examination.

The Good, the Bad and the Dead: A few years ago I completed a case where the parties were arguing over the sale of a funeral home. The depositions were something special as the attorneys were given a crash course on how the funeral business operates. The attorneys were treated to all sorts of information the average person would rather not know such as: Did you know that sometimes funeral homes rent out their chapels to other funeral homes so that a body can be exhibited there? Did you know that there are shops where a funeral director can pick up a body pre-embalmed? Did you know that when funeral directors aren't actually handling a particular funeral they are usually hanging around hospitals waiting for people like you and me to die? The best part of the deposition was how I got there. My client did not pick me up in a hearse, which is essentially a converted limousine. I should only have been so lucky. He picked me up in the van that they use to drive around town picking up dead bodies (sort of like the push-cart used in "Monty Python and the Holy Grail"—"Bring out your dead"). The van stank of formaldehyde. I hope not to be in that van again: not for a very long time. Another amazing aspect of the deposition was the fact that both of my clients (2 funeral directors) were grossly obese. These gentlemen were in their early 50's. Now, I am carrying a few extra pounds myself, but the one client was pushing three hundred pounds and the other was four hundred and fifty pounds. And, they both smoked cigarettes. Wouldn't you think that people who are surrounded by death on a daily basis would want to take better care of themselves so that they don't end up in the box prematurely?

Proper communication with a client is at the heart of the attorney/client relationship, and now is as good a time as any to broach the topic.[23] This is almost always the major bone of contention between attorneys and their clients. Miscommunication and failure of communication result in the overwhelming number of grievances filed against attorneys each year. The problem lies with both the attorneys and the clients. Clients would like to believe that they can pick up a telephone and call their attorney any hour of the day or night, get through to their attorney immediately and spend whatever time they feel they want to spend with the attorney going over whatever issues they choose to discuss. This would work very well in a perfect World. However, in the real World, the attorney is generally handling hundreds of cases simultaneously. If the attorney is asked to stop what he or she is doing all day long to have the same discussions over and over with the same clients, obviously the attorney will not get anything else done. I have found that the best way to head off the mad telephoning client is to try to

---

23.   Such as asking your client not to pick you up in a funeral van.

determine who these people are at the outset of the relationship and then very politely ask them to hire a different attorney. In the event the initial screening process doesn't work, I will advise the client that the client has two choices: (1) I can spend the entire day on the telephone with the client in which case I will most certainly get nothing accomplished on her case, or, (2) I can actually work on the client's case. Most clients get it. Some don't. What follows are some examples of how communication can become a rub between attorneys and their clients.

Sometimes an attorney's clients don't call the attorney on the telephone, but the attorney wishes they would. I once represented several clients who all lived or worked within walking distance of my office. Not a day went by that at least one or two of these clients would simply show up at my office unannounced and plant himself or herself in front of my desk, expecting me to drop whatever I was doing to hear his or her tale of woe. One of these clients would swipe all of the mints and candies in our firm reception area, which were supposed to be for all the clients (the client who ate all our candy had diabetes). Another client would call and pick my brains for half an hour and then show up at the office five minutes later to go over the whole thing again face-to-face. When another of these "droppers-inners" (as I like to call them) would come by, all of my other clients and my secretary would run out of the office, since this gentleman rarely showered or bathed.[24] A fourth dropper-inner was a three hundred fifty pound bearded woman.[25] The moral of the story is to try to represent clients who cannot so easily get physical access to your office. Try to stay away from the "store-front" style of office.

Attorneys are equally guilty when it comes to the breakdown of communication between themselves and their clients. There are plenty of attorneys in the profession who return no one's telephone calls, including clients and adversaries. Or, these attorneys return phone calls so long after the fact that the matter is either no longer relevant or completely forgotten. The attorneys who never or rarely return their client's phone calls are usually the same ones who do not return adversaries' phone calls either. They are as disliked by other attorneys as they are by their own clients. These attorneys will eventually die and be mourned by a room full of empty chairs.

In a novel case of the client going the extra mile to get the attorney's attention, I offer the following. A colleague was hired by a client to handle a rather small

---

24. You guessed it: this was Neil.
25. Neil's sister.

legal matter. The client sent the attorney a modest retainer for the case: $1,500.00. After not hearing from the attorney about the case *for a few days*, instead of calling the attorney for an update on the status of the matter, the client simply called the police and told them that the attorney had stolen his money. After convincing the police that he hadn't stolen any money from anyone, the attorney was finally able to speak with the client. The client told him that he assumed since he had not heard from the attorney for a few days, that the attorney had stolen his money.

As a rule of thumb, I always let my clients know when I am going to be out of the office for more than a few days so that they don't go into panic mode. On one occasion, I took a trip to Florida for a week, and I advised all my clients that I would be out of the office. The trip happened to encompass Christmas and New Years' Eve. I specifically told a client whose case was proceeding nicely on the trial calendar, but for whom no work was due, where I would be and for how long. I gave him a very specific status report a day or two before I left for Florida. On Christmas Eve, I checked my messages only to discovery four messages from the same client, all left within a 2 hour period. Message Number 1: "Please give me a call when you get a chance." Message Number 2: "Why haven't you called me yet?" Message Number 3: "Jesus Christ, are you ever going to call me?" Message Number 4: "I am going to the Grievance Committee if you don't call me immediately." When I called the client and spoke with him—a mere 2 hours after the *first* message—he very calmly told me it was nothing important, he just wanted to know how his case was going ...—On Christmas Eve?

It is clear that the attorney and client must reach a happy medium in communications. Sometimes, the attorney and the client are *communicating* just fine; however, they are simply not *understanding* each other. I recently had to appear at the deposition of a client, which was to take place approximately 300 miles from my office and roughly the same distance from the client's residence. On Monday morning, I advised the client that the deposition would take place "Next Thursday". I gave her the date and the place, and I told her I would meet with her prior to the deposition to prepare for it. Unbeknownst to me, the client took "Next Thursday" to mean three days following our phone conversation on this Monday, so she and two members of her family drove to the opposing attorneys' office: a trip of 300 miles, and about 5 hours of driving. At 5:00 o'clock in the afternoon of "This Thursday", I was informed by my adversary that he had my clients sitting in his reception area under the impression that their deposition was to take place that day. The moral of the story: sometimes no matter what you tell clients, they will find some way to get it wrong.

Sometimes an attorney will do anything to get rid of a client. A colleague had clients run out of her office one day, after noticing mice scurrying around the reception area. The story has a nice ending though: the attorney didn't want the clients around anyway. She also adopted a cat from the local animal shelter to patrol the office for mice and other assorted vermin. She subsequently fell in love with the cat, and took it to her home, where it lives happily ever after for the rest of its nine lives. As for the mice, they have apparently found better places to hide.

Not to be outdone, another colleague had clients run out of his Bronx office after seeing large rats climbing in and out of the bookshelves amongst the law books. Perhaps the rats were attempting to educate themselves in the law. Some day these very same rats may be joining the ranks of first year law students at some fine institution of higher learning.

Had I thought of it, I would have used the rat technique on two clients I represented several years ago. One client, a woman, lived and worked up the road from my office. Over the course of a year and a half, during which I represented this client in connection with a personal injury case, not one day went by that this client did not call me 3 to 5 times each day. Should I have failed to return any one of these calls within fifteen minutes of the client having placed the call, she would simply show up at my office. Each day, I would answer the same questions over and over and over again. There was no keeping this crazy person out of my office. She was of the apparent belief that my office was her second home for the duration of the case. I should have charged her rent.

Not to be outdone, I once represented a gentleman who would also call me multiple times each day to ask the same questions over and over and over again. This gentleman was one step better than the woman previously discussed because he would show up at my office sometimes as early as 6 am, if I decided to come to the office early to catch up on work. He was also known to show up on Saturdays and Sundays. It got to the point where I would have to park my car up the street—so that this client wouldn't see my car in the firm parking lot—and I would have to work with the blinds closed shut, front door locked and the office lights out. I have actually been forced to hide under my desk on occasion to avoid clients like this.

The Certifiably "Troubled" Client: A colleague told me about a client he recently represented in a Connecticut case, who was diagnosed as Bipolar, which actually turned out to be one of the woman's lesser problems. He knew at the time he took the case that the client had serious mental and emotional problems. However, he took the case nonetheless because these problems were one of the reasons the case was so attractive. These problems pre-existed a particular incident but were made much worse by the incident which was the subject of the lawsuit. I suppose if one takes on a seriously troubled client one must expect behavior in conformity with the diagnosis. And, did he get it.

This client would call my colleague (who is Jewish) on a regular basis and leave utterly nonsensical, anti-Semitic messages on his answering machine. In between the messages, the attorney would receive e-mails in a similar vein. Over a two year period, he received nearly 100 such phone messages and e-mails. Almost every message would end with a scoffing: "Mazel Tov", "L'Chaim" or "Shabbat Shalom". Some of the more choice commentaries follow:

1. "Mr. J, this is your gentile client, your forgotten gentile client … check way in the back of your gentile files and you'll find me";

2. "… please send a Heil Hitler to Mr. J…. It's too bad the Germans didn't have ovens, you (Mr. J) should have been the first one in them";

3. "… don't forget, it's the countdown before selling the chometz … maybe you should contact Linda, she would be happy to buy some of your chometz, you know, the bread or the utensils";

4. "I'm not having anything more to do with this case, if you want to call anyone, call your local Rabbi …"

5. "What is it, the chosen race doesn't associate with the non-chosen race … maybe you can call me one of these days, unless it's not kosher";

6. "… obviously Mr. J. is in Israel, practicing the Israeli National Anthem … he's obviously on a Kibbutz somewhere in Israel. So maybe you can mazel tov him into calling me …"

7. "Mr. J. rented a car … got on his Super Jew outfit … and by some magic cabal arrived … Mr. J. should have a temple all to himself …"

8. "… maybe when you get this message … as you are sitting in your office scoffing down another kosher meal …"

9. "… Mr. J., I am one of your clients, one of your non-chosen clients … oh, I understand, I'm not one of the chosen people … now where did I read that? Was it Mein Kampf or the Torah … I guess I'll have to read Mein Kampf and read more about the chosen people …"

10. "Hey, scheister, when are you going to get an office, and by the way scheister, when are you going to get a secretary, and by the way scheister, when are you going to return phone calls …"

11. "... I know I'm just a goyim, a chattel, whatever it is your people call me ... because I'm not the chosen ... are we going to get this all complicated ... it's the West Bank, the East Bank, East Jerusalem, West Jerusalem ..."

12. "... don't forget, I want reparations, I want proof of reparations ..."

13. "... I would like to find out his Hassidic majesty's e-mail address ... I'd like to send this vampire an e-mail before sundown when these vampires take their fingers out of their asses and go to temple ...;

14. "... I've been trying to call that fucking, racist pig bastard, Mr. J.... I know he's some kind of secret sect, can you tell me where I can reach his cave in Israel ... this is ridiculous, these fucking Jews are fighting ... I don't want to be involved in the Teitelbaum wars ...";

15. "... I don't like being screwed, maybe Mr. J. and all his Jewish friends like being screwed ...";

16. "... to solve this whole problem, I think we should take the money and we should send it to Hamas, because they're the only ones that can be legitimately involved in this ... we should send the money to support the Palestinians in their right to exist ...";

17. "... if you want to work it out, talk to your Rabbi ... if this is something that has to be resolved in some Rabbinical counsel ... maybe this is something you need to resolve in the Sanhedrin ...";

18. "... if you need to get ahold of your lawyer ... ha, ha, ha ... give me the name of his Rebbe ...";

19. "... I would like to find out what's going on with the Shekkel wars ...";

20. "... I want to be in court, because I've got to be there to control these fucking Jews ... you can't give these sleazebags any inch of a doubt ...";

21. "... I feel like I'm living in the Gaza Strip ... hopefully the U.N. will protect me ...";

22. "... What, Are you going to lie your way out of this one too ... is that what the Talmud tells you? Oh wait, it does, screw the gentiles, right there black and white in the Talmud ... so you obey that over the U.S. Constitution ... well if you don't agree with it, move out of the country, go where the Talmud is the rule of law";

23. "... Jesus ... I know I shouldn't say that word, I know how it offends you ... oy, Yahweh, protect me ...";

24. "... isn't Satan (Mr. J.) morally and ethically disfigured? ... do wish scumbag-liar a smashed shofar for the high pig days."

The client referred to my friend and colleague alternately as "Racist Pig", "Pig-man", "Shekkelmann", and "Satan", just to mention a few. The most comical aspect of this scenario was that my friend is not at all religious. Yet, the client obsessed over this person as though he were the leader of a Hassidic or Orthodox community.

The Certifiably Insane Potential Client that I didn't take as a client: I once had a prospective client come to my office making the claim that he was being mercilessly tracked down by numerous branches of the federal government. He told me that the FBI, NSA and CIA were all hunting him down for reasons he didn't explain. According to the prospective client, his telephone calls were being wiretapped; he was being followed; and, his life was generally being made miserable by the United States Government. He couldn't articulate why this was happening to him. When I asked if he had any proof upon which we could base our case, he walked into my conference room and fanned out his "proof" on the conference table. The "proof" resembled the cover of the famous Beatles' "Sgt. Pepper's Lonely Hearts Club Band" album. What this person had done was put together a collage of photographs and newspaper clippings and glued these items to a large sheet of construction paper, in no particular order. The "document", for lack of a better word, contained photographs of famous persons all jumbled together, such as Richard Nixon, Billy Joel, Bono, Golda Meir, Mohandas Ghandi, Pope John Paul, II, and the like. Superimposed upon the document were objects such as the Pillsbury Dough Boy, the Michelin Man, Herman Munster and Morris the Cat.

I excused myself (in an effort to control the laughter) and then returned to the room and told the prospective client that his case did not quite appear to be something I could help him with. God only knows what mental institution this gentleman is now confined to.

The Never Gets out of your Face Client: A colleague and friend recently represented a woman who ceaselessly called him over and over again regarding an absolutely absurd case my friend had agreed (in a weak moment) to handle for her. The case had no real value whatsoever, but the client was obsessed with the case, believing it was worth nearly $500,000.00. The woman constantly micromanaged my friend's law practice, second-guessing everything he did, or didn't do. Following her deposition, she continued to call on a daily basis to "discuss" her deposition, including the things she said, or meant to say, or the things she wished she had said (as if any of this had any relevance). The best part of the story is that the woman complained about my friend to her father, who was friendly with the older lawyer who had referred this piece of junk case to my friend. The father called the older lawyer and complained about my friend, who in turn called my friend and gave him a dressing down. In other words, my friend was reported to the principal.

The "Nobody Nose" the Trouble I've seen Client: Another colleague handled a case for a woman who was completely obsessed with her nose. She underwent a procedure which resulted in an ever-so-slight deviation in her nose. She, like the woman above, called this attorney incessantly, not only about the value of her case, but constantly asking if there was anything the attorney could do about her nose—as if the attorney were an ears, nose and throat surgeon.

The Hell Hath No Fury as the Woman Scorned Client: I once represented a woman in a property distribution battle against another woman, with whom she had had a relationship. In short, she was dumped in favor of yet another woman. This woman called me ceaselessly asking the same questions over and over again. No matter what answer I gave this woman, she refused to accept it. Worse yet, she refused to cease having dealings with her former girlfriend. There was nothing I or my adversary could do to keep these former lovers apart. Each time they got together there was another cat fight. And, every time there was a cat fight, I got a call from my opposing counsel. This happened on an almost daily basis. The women owned a house together. At one point, my client was living in one bedroom, and the other two women (my client's former lover and the other woman's new lover) were living in another bedroom—in the same house! On top of that, the other woman's daughter (yes, she had been married to a man at some point) was living in the house with these three warring women. They fought over the use of the swimming pool. They fought over clothing. They fought over furniture. They fought over the telephone bill. They fought over the electric bill. They fought over toaster ovens, and dishwashers. They fought over everything. Something told me not to take this case from its inception. I foolishly did. Fortunately, after much blood-shed, the case finally settled and I hope to never hear from this person again as long as I shall live.

The Hell Hath No Fury as the Man Scorned Client: I once represented a gentleman who had dumped his male partner in favor of another gentleman. This was even worse than the situation described above. The client was stalked by the former boyfriend, who left some of the most bizarre messages on his answering machine I have ever heard. This was clearly not "G" rated material.

9

The Bench: The Seat of Wisdom or The Seat of Your Pants?

The judicial system consists of basically two types of judges: Type A: those with political connections who happen to be attorneys and also happen to be fairly intelligent; and, Type B: those with political connections who happen to be attorneys and also happen to be rather unintelligent. The latter category comes in two distinct varieties: those who, although not particularly intelligent, have a genuine desire to work, or, at least, a genuine desire to appear as though they are working so as to further their additional political objectives; and, those who have given up all pretence of working, are content with what and whom they are, and believe that a paycheck from the public coffers is their divine right. The common thread running through the underpinnings of the bench is most unfortunately, politics. Contrary to the general public's widely-held belief, judges are not "selected" by some sage process whereby members of the legal community having the most skill and experience in the Courtroom are ultimately "elevated" to the bench. Hiram Menzow, a recently deceased trial lawyer, who for a short time in his 80 year career, was a judge; always told people that "'A judge is someone who knows a Governor.'" By God, was he right!

There are two ways to become a judge[1]: by election of the general public, and by appointment, usually by the Governor of the State. To become an elected judge, one needs the endorsement of a major political Party: hopefully the Party in power in the community wherein the election is to be held. So, for example, if one wishes to become a judge in Bronx County, New York, one must run on the Democratic Party ticket. Unlike other political candidates, *however, the Party endorsement is usually the end of the game for judges.* Judicial elections are one of

---

1. The selection process for federal judges is different. All federal judges are appointed by the President of the United States, subject to the "advice and consent" of the Senate.

the rare instances where the actual election is less hard fought than the primary elections. Judicial candidates will fight it out, for example, for the Democratic nod in Bronx County, New York, but the winner of the primary can usually rest easy from that point on. Often times the weaker Party in the district will simply go ahead and cross-endorse the other Party's candidate, and that's it. You are a judge. The actual popular election becomes an event of little consequence, somewhat akin to the unanimous vote received each time Saddam Hussein used to run for re-election.

The members of the profession have known all about this manner of doing business for a long time. But, to hear it from the politicians themselves was somewhat of a revelation to the public: and a vindication to the bar. In December of 2002, three Democratic politicians participating in a program on "How to be a Judge", given to the New York City Bar Association, told the audience that the best way to become a judge in New York is to get involved in politics. The audience was told that lawyers volunteering at political functions are "appreciated" and that party leaders are "very, very aware" of the contributions made by such lawyer volunteers.

Contrary to popular belief, there is no real training of judges prior to election; In fact, there is practically no criteria for becoming a judge in the State of New York other than that one must be an attorney duly admitted to practice law in the State in order to become a justice of the Supreme Court. In New York, the "Supreme Court" is not the highest court in the State, as one would expect. It is the general trial court. One may still hold the position of a town or village justice in the State, without a law degree. I have personally appeared in court before a plumber, a fireman, a grammar school janitor and other non-attorneys sitting as justices. With the exception of the fireman (who was an arrogant buffoon), I have found these justices to be quite capable of performing their functions.

It is not unheard of for judges to be elected who have very little, or no, trial experience. In the wonderful World of Television judges are the very seat of wisdom: they always render correct rulings on objections at trial and always render a fair, impartial and equitable decision: The "fair and equitable" decision being in favor of the stars of the particular show. *In the more mundane World of our American system of justice, judges make plenty of errors.* Some of these errors can be corrected on appeal because they are so blatant that the appellate courts (these are courts which sit in judgment over the decisions of the trial courts) simply must save face by reversing such errors. Other errors are not as blatant, therefore the appellate courts can wash their hands of these matters under the doctrine of "Harmless Error". This last doctrine is the appellate court's way of saying: "We know the trial court judge screwed up, but we've seen worse, so we are not going to do anything about it".

As we have already seen, in order to become a judge, one must obtain a good, solid political endorsement. But how does one go about doing that? Quite simple actually: Political endorsements are given to those who curry favor with the powers that be in the ruling Political Party. So the first thing the prospective judge must do is to find out who it is who really runs the show behind the scenes with the "target" Party. That's the easy part. The harder part is to ingratiate oneself with the power person. This means attending a lot of boring meetings and functions, shaking lots of hands, attending lots of dull functions, eating lots of rubber chickens, runny eggs, and other over or undercooked delicacies. None of the foregoing is particularly hazardous to the general public. Things get a bit sticky, however, when one considers that the newly-elected judge is expected to "take care" of the people who got him or her elected. This means that the political power person (virtually always a practicing attorney), and his cronies, will unquestionably have an advantage over other attorneys appearing before that particular judge. Furthermore, individual judges do not function in a vacuum. They talk to each other just like other co-workers in a firm or corporate setting. They eat lunch together. Political favoritism tends to get around the courthouse. A friend of one judge tends to become a friend of all the judges. An enemy of one judge … you can fill in the blank.

How do judges return these "favors"? Quite simple really: The more obvious manner is by giving lucrative appointments to the attorneys to whom the judge is beholden. The most obvious methods are the trusteeships and guardianships awarded in the cases of deceased or incapacitated persons. Attorneys make a lot of money, with very little work, when they are appointed trustee or guardian of an estate. These positions essentially entail a good deal of paperwork, which can be handled by a good legal secretary or paralegal. Accounting work must also be done, but this can be handled by a separately retained accountant. Investment or custodial work is generally handled by a bank or other financial institution. Rest assured, these are very lucrative appointments. These appointments are not given out by the judges to a random group of qualified attorneys. *They are given out consistently to those attorneys who assisted the judge with his or her campaign as well as friends, relatives and other assorted cronies.* Everyone in the judicial system knows that this practice has gone on for many years, but no one has made any serious effort to end it. Besides, who would take such an initiative; the judges, the lawyers or the Legislature, whose members are mostly lawyers, or the lobbyists, whose members are also mostly lawyers?

The more discrete manner of favoritism falls under the rubric of the "sound discretion of the judge". There are many things which occur at trial and during pre-trial which are held by the appellate courts to be within the sound discretion of the assigned judge. These include the ability of the judge to forgive lateness and defaults. It also includes the ability of the judge to determine who is telling the truth and who is not, when a case is tried to the judge, without a jury. Appellate courts will not touch these issues with a ten foot pole, unless, of course, the error is so blatant that even the appellate court would appear ignorant if it permitted such error to stand.

Here's an example of the latter category. The "hearsay" rule essentially prohibits a party from introducing into evidence an out of court statement for the purpose of proving the truth of the particular statement. But one of the many exceptions to the hearsay rule is that admissions of a party to the lawsuit may be introduced into evidence. An exception recognized by specific statute in the State of New York expressly permits the introduction into evidence of testimony given under oath by a party to the lawsuit. In the course of a trial I recently handled, the trial judge refused to permit the testimony of the defendant in the lawsuit given under oath at a deposition, wherein the defendant had made crucial admissions about the case. The judge's rationale was that she had never heard of any such evidentiary rule: this after I provided the judge with the statute book containing the rule. In other words, I handed her the rule book. On appeal, the appellate court was constrained to reverse because the error was so blatant. There are only two possibilities here: the trial judge had virtually no trial experience either as a sitting judge or as a trial attorney so she really didn't know the rule, or when confronted with the plain language of the rule, she simply could not comprehend what she was reading. Either way, this should be a sobering prospect for any litigant in her courtroom.

Here's another stellar example of fine judicial intellect. I recently attended what is known as a continuing legal education seminar. These are generally referred to as "CLE" seminars. In New York nowadays, as in several other States, an attorney must attend refresher courses in the law as a condition to keeping his or her license to practice.[2] This particular course involved evidence. A panel of eight or nine current sitting judges was formed and I was asked to cross-examine an exemplar witness. The judges were, for the most part, fairly recently elected or appointed judges, although the panel also consisted of a few more experienced

---

2.   This is, of course, at the expense of the attorney: putting an inordinate burden on sole practitioners.

jurists. Every single judge but one found objectionable the following question: "Did you [witness] discuss your testimony today with anyone prior to testifying here?" The judges were all of the belief that this question elicited a hearsay response. However, it is fairly obvious that the correct response to the question is either Yes or No. No hearsay statement is requested by the question, and the question is therefore not objectionable. *Only one judge out of the nine knew the correct answer.* These were real sitting judges. These weren't television judges such as Judge Judy or Judge Joe. This should be a rather frightening thought.

The foregoing is not the type of rulings we generally see on "The Practice" or the old "Perry Mason" television programs. However, these types of ridiculous rulings are made on a daily basis in our Courtrooms around the Nation. *The bottom line: Don't assume it is right just because the judge said so.*

Other Judicial Gems: One of our favorite county court judges in New York was most recently a lower court judge. While sitting at the lower court she developed a reputation for being completely unreasonable, biased and generally unintelligent. I appeared before this judge on two occasions while she sat on the lower court bench. The first occasion was a situation where the landlord was being sued by the tenant for not turning over possession of an apartment precisely on the first day of the month. The landlord could not turn over the apartment until the 7th day of the month (a mere 6 days later than scheduled) because the landlord could not get the prior tenant to leave on time. Anticipating this problem, the landlord put the appropriate clause into the new lease to the effect that the landlord cannot be sued by the new tenant for failure to deliver possession of the premises by the first of the month. This judge, after reading the lease (and having this particular provision pointed out to her) granted judgment immediately in favor of, not the landlord, but instead, the tenant! The second time I appeared before this brilliant member of the bench involved a traffic offense—my client was accused by a local police officer of speeding. This type of case is fairly simple. If the arresting officer fails to show up at court, the judge is supposed to dismiss the case because of the constitutional principle that every accused person has the right to confront his or her accuser. The police officer is the accuser, and it is only fair, from a constitutional standpoint, to permit the accused the right to question the officer under oath. This is simple enough. If the arresting officer does show up to court most people do not realize it but the officer has the authority to reduce the charge in exchange for a guilty plea to a lesser offense and the waiver of a trial. The courthouse then becomes somewhat like the old Monty Hall television program, "Let's make a deal". You go out to the hallway, you speak with the officer and you try to get your speed knocked down to a lower speed, or possibly to a non-speeding violation. The courts encourage this because they certainly do not want to have a trial in every traffic case coming before them on a given day. If a judge spends a mere fifteen minutes on each traffic trial, and he or she has to hear fifty trials: you can do the math. The judge will be on the bench all day and night.

This day, however, I knew I was in trouble when the arresting officer told me outside the courtroom (after looking around at his fellow officers and chuckling) "You have never been before this judge on a traffic case, have you?" "I'd love to help you but ..." The judge then started off the call of her calendar (this is simply a role call of the cases) with the following comments: "This is how I handle my cases. Those of you who pleaded "Not Guilty" to the traffic charges, I am sure are in fact "guilty". I do not accept plea agreements. You have to own up to your guilt, and if you do I may, just may, have some leniency toward you. But if you make me go through a trial only to result in your being found guilty, I will not be lenient. I do not accept plea agreements. Your best bet is to change your plea right now to "Guilty", and ask for leniency". And I had always thought that a criminal defendant was presumed innocent until proven guilty in our American judicial system. Not so for this judge. As a reward for this type of fine judicial craftsmanship, this judge was elevated to a higher court level where she sits in judgment over felony cases. That means that this judge has the authority to sentence someone up to life in prison without parole. From all indications she has maintained the same attitude and is essentially as stupid today as she was in the past. Both defense counsels and prosecutors fear to step foot in her courtroom, and, of course, nobody does anything about it. No one complains because no one wants to buck the system. Also, no one wants to be the attorney who complains about a judge, and then ends up appearing before that judge some time down the line.

A colleague recently handled a personal injury trial in New York. As he was approaching the judge's chambers, he heard laughing and guffawing emanating from the room. When he entered, he saw the judge sitting at one end of a desk and an attorney, casually dressed sitting at the other end with his feet up on the desk. The attorney was to be his adversary at trial. The clerk of the court then told my friend that this other attorney had yet to lose a trial before this particular judge. As one can imagine, every objection made by my colleague at trial was overruled, and the judge ruled in the other attorney's favor throughout the trial. The end result was exactly what one would expect: my colleague lost the case. Following the dismissal of the case, my colleague told the judge politely that it appeared that the judge had gone out of his way to make the case difficult for him to win. The next day, an order appeared on the attorney's desk, seeking to hold him in contempt of court. Thus, when all was said and done, justice was denied the client, and the attorney found himself defending against contempt charges: all because he stood up for his client's right to a fair trial against an obviously biased judge. This judge has since been forced to retire because the judicial powers that be would not support his remaining on the bench.

In the "Nice Guy Charlie" category, is the federal judge who insisted that an attorney appear before him the day after the attorney's father suddenly passed away. The distraught attorney pleaded with the judge to adjourn the court date to another day. This judge was of the opinion that the request was asking a bit too much of his lordship, and he refused to grant the adjournment. The attorney, instead of appearing in court, remained with his family and did not attend the meaningless court conference. As a result, both he and his partner were assessed $50,000 in sanctions, which were subsequently entered as a money judgment against the two attorneys, and proceedings were brought to enforce the judgment against the personal assets of the attorneys. Instead of being paid to handle the case, the two-person law firm ended up having to pay a $50,000 bill to the court. All in all, it was a very expensive funeral for dad.

I once handled an eviction proceeding on behalf of a landlord in one of the local, justice courts.[3] The eviction proceeding was scheduled for trial the very next evening. The tenant's attorney filed a lawsuit in federal court against the landlord on the basis of what is referred to as "Diversity Jurisdiction". There is a strong principle carried down from the origins of our system that federal courts are supposed to stay out of purely "local" matters. Federal courts can only hear cases when there is what is called "Federal Question Jurisdiction", meaning that issues in the case involve federal statutes or the federal Constitution, or the federal courts may hear cases involving something called "Diversity Jurisdiction". Diversity occurs when all the parties on one side of the transaction are from a different State than all the parties on the other side of the transaction, and the parties are fighting over more than $75,000.00. In our case, there was clearly Diversity Jurisdiction since the only plaintiff resided in New York State and the only defendant resided in another State. However, landlord tenant eviction cases are strictly local matters to be heard in the lower State courts: not in federal courts.

Nonetheless, the Federal judge granted, *ex parte*, an injunction halting all action in the local court. An "*ex parte*" action is taken by the courts in the absence

---

3.   These are the successor courts to the old Justices of the Peace.

of one of the parties to the lawsuit and is sometimes done on an emergency basis. On the day that the judge granted the *ex parte* injunction, the judge happened to be sitting in the courtroom of a different judge, on a different floor of the court- house. I arrived at the correct courtroom fifteen minutes early, only to find out (five minutes late) that the judge just happened to be sitting in the other judge's courtroom that morning. Apparently, the two judges were going to a luncheon later in the day and they wanted to leave together. By the time I arrived at the correct courtroom (which, of course, was not really this judge's courtroom) the injunction had already been granted. There is, of course, what I shall refer to as "the sleaze factor" here in that my adversary should very well have expected me to have been in the other courtroom and should have asked the judge to have his court officers check that courtroom when I did not appear on time. Be that as it may, when I got to see the judge (albeit five minutes after the appointed time), the judge candidly admitted to me that he had indeed signed the injunction but he did not realize that he was halting a trial of the eviction proceeding in a local court. *In other words, he didn't really read the papers.* He had no idea whatsoever what he had signed or ordered. Naturally, the judge refused to do anything about changing his decision. It was too much trouble and he didn't want to be late for his luncheon. So, if you think the high and mighty federal judges do not make mistakes, think again.

Another Federal Blunder: I once handled a case against an attorney who was attempting to wrestle a business away from one of his own clients. After two days of hearings in the case, the federal judge called all parties into his chambers (this is an office room where the judge sits when he is not in his courtroom). The judge wanted the case settled because, at this stage of the game, he was tired of lis- tening to both the plaintiff and the defendant. My co-counsel and I continued our impassioned plea concerning the manner in which this attorney went about systematically attempting to wrestle the business away from his own client, after the client had hired the attorney to protect the very business the attorney was now attempting to seize. After two days of hearings; and, after an hour's confer- ence; the Judge tells us: "'Surely you don't mean to be impugning the character of the attorney.'" That was exactly what we were attempting to do. God forbid we should impugn the character of an attorney who was trying to steal from his own client. The judge never got it.

This particular judge was pushing 80 years of age at the time of the trial. In my opinion, judges of advanced years should be removed from the federal bench once it is quite apparent that senility has set in. In case you didn't know, federal judges are not elected for terms. They are appointed by the President of the

United States, with the advice and consent of the Senate.[4] They hold their positions essentially for as long as they continue to breathe and don't fall face-first from the bench. But don't hold your own breath waiting for them to voluntarily retire.

Some of the most colorful judges are those who sit in the city, town and village courts. The personalities of these judges range from A to Z. A standing joke in the New York legal community was that justice in the Yonkers City Court really was blind, because at one time this Court had not one, but two legally blind judges sitting on the bench. In another Westchester County justice court the local justice simply could not be heard. The justice's voice was so low that no one could hear or understand a word he said. The standing joke being that justice was dumb in the Mount Pleasant Justice Court.

Many of the local courts have more than one sitting justice. In one Northern Westchester, New York court the sitting male justice can clear out a courtroom of 100 or more litigants, including criminal cases, in less than 45 minutes. The female justice formerly sitting in the very same court could take 45 minutes to dispose of one case. The local attorneys, of course, pick up on this sort of thing so they try to work it so that their cases will be heard by the faster of the two justices. This is called "Judge Shopping".

Some of the justices have absolutely no sense of humor, while others are hard to take seriously. One recently retired justice in Northern Westchester County, New York used to keep a miniature violin by his bench, which he would pretend to play when he thought someone was telling him an unbelievable story. Another justice trades one-liners with the litigants and spectators in his courtroom on a regular basis.

Then, there are the downright mean and nasty judges. These are the guys (always men) who the attorneys just want to either retire or do us a big favor and die. Of course, they never do either. They seem to hang around forever. In this category are judges such as one in Brooklyn who was prone to courtroom tirades about the lack of experience and knowledge of the attorneys appearing in his courtroom. He well earned the nickname prefix "Hollering". There is another judge whose demeanor almost perfectly matches his name, hence he has been given the nickname by us attorneys: "Nasty". He is alternatively known as "Count Dracula" as a result of his extremely long canine teeth, hanging half-way

---

4.   In recent times we have seen the Senate abuse this "advice and consent" authority by essentially creating a veto power over the President's selections for federal judges.

down his lower lip. It might as well be a reference to the fact that he can suck the life blood out of an attorney and the attorney's case.

This nick-name giving is all behind the back sort of stuff. To the judge's face, the attorney must always say "Your Honor" or "Judge", even if the judge is the most despicable, dishonorable and vicious character on the planet.

10

The Court personnel: clerks, secretaries and other un-elected decision-makers

If you have been practicing for some time you know that much of what goes on in the courthouse on a given day is dictated by the clerical staff. Contrary to popular belief, most courthouses are not buildings where you walk in off the street directly into a particular judge's courtroom. Most of the square footage of the typical courthouse is allotted to the enormous staff, of clerks and secretaries, who are responsible for the mechanics of sorting out mountains of paper involved from the filing of a lawsuit up until, and beyond, the day of trial or settlement of the case. In between the levels of administration and offices, one will find the various courtrooms assigned to the judges. *The judges in the courthouse are far outnumbered by the clerical workers.*

Generally speaking, each sitting judge maintains a law secretary or law clerk, who is an attorney working full-time for the judge. In many instances it is this person, rather than the judge, who actually reads the applications (motions and the like), and renders decisions in connection with the multitude of applications made to the Court on a given day. Judges are, of course, supposed to render all decisions according to constitutional mandate. However, since there are so few judges in relation to the vast number of cases pending in the court at any given time, the court system does its best to keep the judges actually presiding over trials for as much of their work-time as possible. After all, as much as it would assist in reducing the case backlogs, the judicial system will not go so far as to seat someone on the bench to conduct a trial, if that person is not actually an elected or appointed judge. This does not change the fact that the law secretaries and law clerks wield a great deal of authority nonetheless. Most judges simply do not have the time to preside over trials and also cull through the thousands of pages of applications submitted to them each week. Therefore, the judges usually have the law secretary or the law clerk go through the applications, and then make a rec-ommendation to the judge as to how that person thinks the application should be decided. As you can imagine, these recommendations hold a lot of weight and are not lightly tossed aside. Some judges simply allow their law secretaries to review the applications, make the decisions, and then affix the judge's stamped signature to the end of the decision. No judge will admit to this but the practice is fairly common.

These law secretaries and law clerks also conduct conferences, which are essen-tially meetings amongst the attorneys in a particular case to find out where the parties stand with respect to the time periods they have been given to get their cases ready for trial. Some more aggressive law secretaries or law clerks are very good mediators and have been known to effectuate settlements as a result. All of this is encouraged, because the judges cannot be in more than one place at a time, and because the court system keeps strict statistics as to the number of cases filed, the number of cases assigned to a particular judge, and the speed at which the judges can dispose of cases. For the most part, the judicial system is not very interested *in how* the dispositions come about or whether some equitable concept of "justice" is achieved. In other words, nobody really gives a damn whether the party in the right wins the case or loses. The goal of the judicial system is to get the cases closed out—and fast. If this means throwing out meritorious cases in the name of expediency, so be it.

The other important personnel at the court are the clerks. There are several different types of clerks. The general rule of thumb is that the larger the popula-tion of the County in which the court sits, the more intricate the level of the clerk bureaucracy. For instance, in Putnam County, New York there is "The Court Clerk". This clerk does it all: one-stop shopping, so to speak. The advantage of the one court, one clerk scenario is that the right hand usually knows what the left hand is doing: at least when they are both attached to the same body. In the case of Putnam County, New York the system works very well. The one clerk happens to be very, very good at what he does. The same does not hold true, for example, in Kings County, New York[1]. There are few court bureaucracies like unto that of Kings County. Not only is there a clerk for every single paper anyone would ever need or want to file in a judicial proceeding, but one usually must negotiate one's way through several layers of clerks in order to get anything filed in this court. These clerks are essentially unelected, informal lawmakers because

---

1.   The term itself "Kings" County causes one to wonder what monarch in his correct
      frame of mind would want to live or work in Brooklyn.

your entire case depends upon whether or not the clerk of the day decides to accept or reject your proffered papers. There is no uniformity in this court. Whether your papers are accepted or rejected on any given day depends upon what clerk happens to be assigned to Window Number 45 that day, and whether or not he or she has had a bad night or a good night's sleep. Rule of thumb: All papers to be filed in the regal, County of Kings, should be given to someone from the area, who is friendly with a fair number of the clerks. Papers should not be sent there blindly: they are virtually certain to be rejected. The cute thing about these clerks is the sadistic manner in which they reject papers offered for filing. If the clerk finds five items which he perceives to be mistakes in your papers, he will not point these five (5) items out to you when he first rejects your papers. He will reject your papers five times: each time giving you a different reason why he cannot accept your papers. It's more fun this way because the clerks get to enjoy watching the attorneys scramble to meet deadlines.

Sometimes the clerks will issue their own "pocket veto". They will simply hold your papers until your deadline has passed, and then they will return your papers to you after there is nothing you can do about it. This is a particularly sadistic tactic, utilized well in Brooklyn and Queens Counties. Other times, the clerks will reject your papers for one, two or three different reasons, and then when you finally get the papers together the way the clerk wanted them in the first place, the clerk tells you that the papers are late. The clerk tells you that the papers had to have been filed within a certain number of days after you dated them. Of course, had the clerk accepted the papers the first time you presented them, this wouldn't have been an issue. The clerks in Brooklyn, in particular, love utilizing this tactic.[2]

In addition to the general clerks of the court, each judge has his or her own clerk: usually called a "Part Clerk" in New York State. In most other States, the judge's personal clerk is just referred to as "judge so-and-so's clerk", or the "Courtroom Clerk". You have no choice but to get on this clerk's good side (and stay there) because this clerk knows every vagary of the judge, and will usually advise you—if you ask politely. Rule: be especially nice to the judge's clerk. If the clerk feels you are (I love this new word which has found its way into our vocabulary) "disrespecting" him or her, you are in for all sorts of trouble. Your papers can be mysteriously lost or shuffled to the bottom of the pile of papers to be read. Your case can be pushed to the end of the court's calendar—meaning that you have to sit around doing nothing all day waiting for your case to be heard. Worst of all, you may never get an adjournment of your case when you so desperately need it (and considering how many times attorneys must be in two or more places at the same time, you will need it).

So far, we have been dealing with the run-of-the-mill clerks, who generally could care less about you, as an attorney, unless you manage to either ingratiate yourself with the clerk (good) or you manage to piss him or her off (not good). Unfortunately, the bribe-taking clerks still exist in the profession. The story comes to mind of the attorneys lined up to file papers with a particular clerk in one of the New York City Courts. Each attorney approaches the clerk, shakes the clerk's hand and offers his papers for filing. The clerk gives a huge smile and places the papers in his pile. The young attorney approaches the clerk and hands over his papers. The clerk—without even glancing at the papers—yells at the young attorney that he cannot accept the papers and that "I have no time for you." The young attorney is later approached by an old pro who tells him "You see how everyone is shaking the clerk's hand before they hand over their papers?" "They are handing the Clerk a $20.00 bill".

As one can imagine, New York County (this court covers all persons who live in the Borough of Manhattan), handles quite a few divorce cases. The clerk's office handling divorces in Manhattan is extremely backed-up. It can take a very long time to get your divorce judgment out of the clerk's office once it finds its way down from the judge. People don't like this.[3] In other words, the judge has decided to grant you a divorce. But, the judge's decision is meaningless unless and until the clerk's office enters a paper called a judgment.[4] Not long ago, a

---

2.   The beauty of the court system in New York is the sheer number of rules an attorney must somehow become familiar with. The state promulgates rules, most of which are contained in the Civil Practice Law and Rules and the Uniform Rules for Trial Courts. An attorney simply must know these rules. But, the concept of "Uniform Rules" is a misnomer because one finds out that each County has its own rules and procedures (unpublished); each judge has his or her own rules (published); and, each clerk's office has its own procedures (not published). Sometimes the procedures of the particular clerk's office are actually contrary to the "Uniform Rules", which are state promulgated and are supposed to take precedence. However, if you want the clerk to accept your papers, you had better follow the clerk's particular, albeit unpublished rules. Superimposed upon the foregoing is the fact that individual clerks within the same clerk's office don't always agree on what papers to accept and what papers not to accept, therefore, it is a crap-shoot which clerk you will be confronted with on any given day. Lastly, if the foregoing doesn't have your head spinning already, all of the forgoing rules (published and unpublished) are constantly being changed.

3.   Especially if you are getting re-married and have already booked the catering hall.

group of attorneys and a clerk in the divorce part of the court decided informally that something needed to be done about this. What they did was this: the attorneys began spreading the word, via advertising, that they could obtain divorce judgments much faster than other lawyers. This turned out to be truth in advertising. The attorneys paid off the clerk, who expedited their divorce judgments. It all worked quite well for a while before the authorities got wind of it and the expected arrests were made. The moral of the story: at all cost avoid filing for divorce in Manhattan. Move to another County (preferably outside New York City) and file for divorce there after the expiration of the required waiting period.

The Courthouse facilities

A word is in order about courthouse facilities. So you are going to court? Or so you think. The first thing you need to know is which courthouse and where is your judge sitting. In New York County Supreme Court, there are at least three courthouses of which I am aware. In Westchester County Supreme Court, there are two. Kings County Supreme Court may have the most number of courthouses: there are at least four separate courthouse buildings of which I am aware. Mind you, this is all the same court: just different buildings, each of which can be several city blocks away from the other. You are on your own when it comes to figuring out exactly which building your judge is in. The fun part is that the courtroom administrators like to keep the attorneys on their toes, so they constantly shuffle judges and courtrooms around about as often as you would change your underwear. Today, your case is to be heard by judge A: tomorrow the case is re-assigned to judge B. A week from now, the case will be re-re-assigned to judge

---

4.   The distinction between a decision and a judgment is lost on many attorneys, so I certainly wouldn't expect a non-attorney to be familiar with it. A decision can be verbal or in writing, but it is exactly what one would expect. A judge has ruled, for lack of a better word, in favor of a particular person against another person for a particular reason. The judgment embodies the decision. But the judgment must be in writing and it must be accepted for filing (what is referred to as "entering the judgment") by the clerk's office in order for the decision to have any real effect. I recently had a case in New York County where the trial judge actually signed the judgment, but the judgment clerk made me jumped through many ridiculous hoops to get the judgment entered. One such hoop included a request that the supervising judge of the court sign an order saying basically that it was okay for the judgment clerk to enter the judgment. This is obviously ridiculous since the trial judge's act in signing the judgment does just that.

C. Better yet, today you appear in Room 352 at 360 Adams Street, tomorrow you appear before the same judge, but she is in 120 Schermerhorn Street. Lawyers usually check the New York Law Journal[5] to try to figure out where their judge is going to be on a given day, or whether their case has been re-assigned. However, 50% of the time the Law Journal says one thing but when you get to the court, the court administrators have done something else that very morning. You then find yourself running from building to building trying to locate your judge, who was re-assigned to a new building and/or new courtroom that very same morning. Each time you have to enter another building, you used to have to go through the metal detectors, with their serpentine lines, all over again.[6] By the time you find your judge you are usually late, and exhausted, and you haven't done a stitch of legal work. You also get chastised for lateness.

If the judicial re-assignments and building switches don't get you, the elevators will. It is a general rule of courthouses that elevators never work. If the elevators at the Southern District federal courthouse in Manhattan worked, a longstanding tradition would be broken. I believe it is against some unwritten federal law for these elevators to work: you know, to carry people up and down floors. The elevators in the New York State Courts are not much better. A typical trick is for the courthouse personnel to shut down elevators for maintenance between the hours of 9:00 am and 10:00 am: just when the attorneys are required to be in court, and when we need to use them most desperately.[7]

Courtrooms run the gamut. One would think that the "Supreme Court" facilities (New York State's version of what most other states refer to as their "Supe-

---

5. A particularly droll, but necessary publication attorneys are supposed to read on a daily basis.

6. The Court system finally set up an attorney secure pass so that attorneys who remember to bring their pass with them to the courthouse can breeze through the non-attorneys on the serpentine lines at the metal detectors. This always made me wonder: why is an attorney less likely than a non-attorney to bring a gun to court and attempt to shoot a judge or blow up the building? If anything, the attorneys, who appear before some of these horrific judges and are abused by them on a regular basis, would seem to be more, rather than less, likely to assassinate a judge.

7. If you think we attorneys are too lazy to use the staircase, keep in mind that sometimes we need to be on the 18th floor of the courthouse and we have to lug our 50 pound briefcase with us. Add to this the fact that the courthouse administrators are constantly rotating which doors leading from the stairwells to the inside corridors will be locked on any given day. Thus, you can amble your way all the way up to the 18th floor where your judge is sitting, only to find out that the door to the corridor is locked and the nearest re-entry point is back down on the 12th floor.

rior Court" or "Circuit Court") would be in better physical condition than the local courts (the so-called Justice Courts). Not a chance. While some of the local courts are indeed a run-down mess, for the most part, the local courts are newer buildings, with functioning air conditioning and heat, and pleasant décor.

The Supreme Court facilities are anything but "Supreme". I recall appearing before a Judge in New York County where behind the judge's head where it was impossible to ignore were the letters: "In od we Tust", as opposed to "In God we Trust". Perhaps that's their way of saying that New York County doesn't trust in God or can't spell simple words. The New York County courthouse has plaster raining down on peoples' heads. The ceilings are, for the most part, coming apart. One can wait a half hour for an elevator in New York County. The Bronx County courthouse looks magnificent from the outside, but once inside, you will find more broken chairs, graffiti scribbled on the seats, and enough bubblegum stuck to the floor that it's like feeling your way through a mine field. Some of the Kings County courtrooms look more like a town hall meeting room from Mayberry RFD than a courtroom. The courtrooms are festooned with graffiti and carvings in the wooden seats. I have always wondered: who creates this "artwork", and when do they do it? Is this an "after-hours" project? If so, who does it: The Court Officers? or maybe the cleaning personnel? Or, do the graffiti artists sit there in court carving their boyfriend or girlfriend's name into the seats while the judge is actually sitting on the bench?

Westchester County is in a class by itself. It is one of the newest of the supreme court buildings, and is, without a doubt, in the worst shape. Before the building was even completed lawsuits were being filed (in that very court) against the companies responsible for building it. It is impossible to appear in Westchester Supreme Court on a no-construction day. The courthouse is under a perpetual re-construction project. A fun feature of the construction work is that for a long time when you appeared in Westchester County Supreme Court, there was a different way to enter the courthouse almost each day. Sometimes one could walk through the underground parking garage directly into Door A. Sometimes, one must go to Door B. Sometimes, one was directed outside the garage only to have to go back in again at yet another Door. It's somewhat akin to the old Monte Hall program "Let's Make a Deal". I'll take the courthouse behind door number 3, please.

Other services which rarely work at courthouses would include the photocopy machines and change machines. This is particularly handy when one needs portions of a court file, or needs to photocopy a deed or mortgage and the only place one can get it is at the courthouse or clerk's office. Rest assured that the only available photocopier will not be working, or if it is working, you will not be able to get the change to work it.

11

The Adversary

The Illiterate

One would think after four years of college and three years (four years part-time) of professional school, together with the tremendous amount of reading and writing required for the actual practice of law, that lawyers would be particularly literate. Not so. I have litigated cases against adversaries whose grammar was so poor it was almost impossible to dispute their arguments because you couldn't figure out what it was they were trying to say. I sometimes wondered if they knew what it was they were trying to say. I once had an adversary submit papers to an appellate court wherein he misspelled my client's name six different ways in the same document. He submitted mountains of applications to the court in connection with our several cases: none of which contained anything spelled correctly or sentences that made any sense. He ultimately lost these cases. I understand he has since made several efforts to become a judge. I suppose if he tries hard enough, and garners enough political support, one day he too may be sitting on the bench with some of our more brilliant legal minds.

The Courteous

We all know that the law is a profession of civility, right? Think again. The following is an actual colloquy from the stenographic record of a deposition taken in connection with a personal injury case in New York. This case involved injuries sustained by a roofer as a result of a fall from a roof. Safety equipment (or lack thereof) was the key issue in the case. A deposition is essentially a series of questions posed by the deposing attorney to the person answering the question, who is known as the deponent or witness. The questions are answered under oath before a stenographer or reporter, who transcribes the colloquy. The designation "Q" refers to the question asked by the interrogating attorney and the "A" is the deponent's answer. For our purposes "O" will be the objections raised by the attorney representing the deponent. The deponent in this case was the project manager of the roofing job.

Q. Let me just give you some instructions. You've been sworn in. I assume you understand the nature of the oath you took here this afternoon?

A. I know, I seen Perry Mason.

Q. I'm now asking you to describe the safety harnesses.

A. Like you are going to understand what the Hell I'm talking about.

Q. Well, if I ask a question then you are going to answer.

A. This is stupid now. This is stupid.

Q. Could you answer that please?

A. I answered it twice.

Q. You haven't answered it. Do me a favor; don't raise your voice to me.

A. Don't ask me the question three times.

O. Counsel, sir, this is not an opportunity for you to waste this man's time or for you to repeat the same question five or six times.

Q. Well, let me tell you something.

O. This is not an opportunity for you to harass my client.

Q. I haven't asked that question once. I haven't repeated a single question. If you're not diligent enough that you can't listen to the questions … that's fine. And don't tell me about wasting anybody's time. I accommodated deponent by making a three-hour drive here.

O. You accommodated him by bringing a frivolous lawsuit against him, sir.

Q. You may think it's frivolous. Are we going to decide that now, Mr. O?

O. Sure, let's decide it right now, sign my stipulation.

Q. Why should I?

O. Because you have no basis for suing this man.

Q. Why don't you save your arguments for the judge, not Now.

O. Why don't you stop raising your voice and being obnoxious asking the same questions over and over again.

Q. I resent that.

O. Resent it all the way; I don't care.

Q. Who's wasting your client's time?

O. You are.

Q. Oh really, with your stupid objections.

O. So press on, and make it quick.

Q. I'm going to be here as long as it takes.

O. That's good because you're paying for it anyway in the end.

Q. What difference does that make?

O. Ask your insurer. Ask the Ethics Board.

Q. Don't threaten me, Mr. O.

A. Don't raise your voice in my office.

Q. Don't point your finger at me.

A. You pointed your finger at me; I can point my finger at you.

Q. I didn't.

A. You did again.

O. Ask the question.

A. So let's press on and get this bullshit over with.

(Later on in the deposition....)

Q. In order to take measurements in order to determine a price, did you actually go on the roof at this building?

A. It's the only way you can do it.

Q. And did you walk the entire roof?

A. No, I only walked half of it. Of course I walked the whole roof.

Q. What did you use to measure the roof, sir?

A. A tape measure. What do you use? That's fucking stupid.

Q. (directed to the reporter) Just make sure you're taking this all down, please.

A. Jesus Christ.

Q. Did you take a measurement of the parapet of the roof?

A. Probably.

Q. Was the height of the parapet significant to you either in terms of your bid or any other reason?

A. No idea what you're babbling about.

Q. Did you measure the height of the roof off the ground from the ground up to the beginning of the roof?

A. I mean any moron can look off the roof and tell how high it is within a foot or two.

Q. Could you explain to me generally what your understanding is of "safety netting"?

A. I don't know what you're talking about for the third time. Until you show me what you are babbling about, I can't explain it.

(The deposition proceeds ...)

Q. Did you have a conversation with the plaintiff regarding the accident?

A. Yes.

Q. Did the conversation take place—do you know where it took place?

A. He's brain dead; isn't he (referring to the interrogating attorney)?

(Continuing …)

O. Would you please ask your next question? It's been about five minutes since your last question. Can you please ask your next question?

Q. I will when I'm ready.

O. Well, you know what, you're not entitled to abuse this man (referring to the deponent) and keep him here all day for frivolous questions; you're not.

Q. Please be quiet, Mr. O.

O. Please be quiet, Mr. Q.

Q. This is a different question. I'm trying to help you if I can because you seem to need some help (referring to the deponent).

O. How about returning my phone calls, huh?

Q. What does that have to do with anything?

O. There's a difference between returning a call and not returning a call.

Q. Shut up.

O. Make me.

Q. I would like to.

O. Go ahead and make me.

(Continued …)

O. You can ask fifty more times; you seem to like to do that. However, he's not answering that question. You asked it up and down; you are abusing him. You brought a frivolous lawsuit.

Q. Let's let a judge decide that.

O. You don't seem to understand that this witness was not subject to sub-poena. You don't know how to bring a commission, counsel?

Q. No?

O. No, you don't know how.

Q. I chose not to.

O. We all practice differently. We will see what the court has to say about how you practice. Does your insurer know you're taking risks?

Q. I'm not taking risks. Don't worry about what my carrier is concerned about.

(Continued …)

O. Just ask the next question, counsel.

A. Just let him babble 'til he's tired.

Q. I'm not going to get tired.

A. You're the one that has to drive home, not me.

Q. I've been doing this for twenty-eight years.

O. Still haven't learned.

A. Still practicing.

Q. Mr. O, you wish you could be the lawyer I am.

O. Ask your next question.

Q. Why don't you shut your mouth.

A. We will have none of this in my office.

O. After twenty-eight years, you can't return an attorney's phone call, a couple of calls; that's the way you practice. That's the way you practice. I guess I wish I could be like that; but you know what, I don't.

(Continued …)

Q. Sir, I can probe his recollection.

O. No. No, you asked him paragraph by paragraph. You probed him like a proctologist.

Q. Moron.

O. Excuse me?

Q. You're really a moron.

O. Okay, you've been practicing twenty-eight years; personalized attacks. Did I call you a name?

Q. What name did I call you counsel, sir?

O. Someone who doesn't return my phone calls, that's what I would call you; someone who brings frivolous lawsuits. What else do you want me to call you?

Q. I can call you a lot.

A. You're wasting my time.

Q. Excuse me?

O. Ask your next question, counsel; or call me another name as long as this is on the record.

A. While we are still young.

(Continued with another deponent on the same day … same cast of characters.)

O. Ask a question that doesn't presume. That's called laying a foundation. Twenty-eight years of practice. I know I'm a moron in your eyes, but please ask a proper question.

Q. Did you instruct the workers to use any safety equipment after the plaintiff's accident?

O. Objection, don't answer that.

Q. What's the basis for the objection.

O. Counsel, I've let you go off on tangents all over the place.

Q. Give me—I need a basis for your objection.

O. You need a lot of things, but I'm not going to give you all the things you need.

Q. You can shut up; that's number—

O. You can shut up too. You've had more than enough—

Q. Mr. Deponent [A], don't worry about your lawyer.

O. Don't worry about this attorney, and I use the term loosely. (Continued ...)

Q. You're directing him (deponent) [A] not to answer?

O. Yes. I've been very lenient with you.

Q. You haven't been lenient.

O. Oh, sure I have.

Q. You've done everything you could to prevent me from taking the deposition.

O. You don't know what I can do.

Q. I'm very scared, Mr. O. Fool.

O. Fool, did you just call me a fool?

Q. Yes, I did.

O. I may be asking for sanctions in addition to the sanctions for frivolous lawsuit.

Q. If you're not going to be professional, then shut up.

O. Have I called you any names? What's professional in your judgment, calling names? Ask a question.

Q. Don't tell me what to do.

The following is an actual colloquy from another fun deposition taken in a New York case. This lawsuit involved the collection efforts of a bank against a corporate debtor and its principal, who it is alleged was scheming to hide assets from the bank. The bank's attorney was attempting to find out the relationship of the individual debtor with various corporate entities owned by the debtor's wife.

Q. Do you (debtor) have any understanding or knowledge why PC Corporation pays for your office?

A. Well, I could be nasty about this.

O. Answer the question.

A. Because I need an office to function out of. My wife is kind enough to pay for it.

Q. What functioning do you perform out of your office?

A. I meet with receivers very frequently. I produce records. I spend a lot of time doing that.

Q. What benefit does PC Corporation get from you meeting with receivers and spending all that time?

A. I am great in bed.

Q. Anything else?

A. No. It was a stupid question.

(Continued ...)

Q. I object to your attorney answering these questions. I would instruct you (objecting attorney) to please refrain from doing so. If you have an objection, then make your application. If you are going to instruct your client not to answer, do not answer my questions.

O. I will object to your attempting to intimidate me. Keep your voice at a modulated level. I listen to every word you say. Don't treat me as if I am lower than a snake's belly.

(Continued ...)

Q. I have a right to know his [the witness] ability to testify under oath.

O. He has given you the best of his recollection.

Q. Which may be garbage; I have a right to know if he can testify truthfully.

O. You are assuming, as you told me, that he is a crook and I object to the tenor of your questions, the presumption that my client is stealing money.

(Continued ...)

Q. Is this, your accounting for the money?

A. Excuse me. I am not a lawyer. I don't know what accounting means for the money. To me, that's accounting for the money. I didn't know I had to kiss your ass and show you every time money came in.

Q. Have you answered every question posed of you by the receiver?

A. Whenever he asked a question, yes. I spent ten fucking hours with the man.

Here is a tidbit from another deposition:

Q. Mr. Yates, did you maintain an office in Mr. Abe's premises?

A. You could say so. I was Mr. Abe's investigator.

Q. What type of investigations did you do?

A. I walked his dog. I investigated dog shit.

From yet another deposition

"He's (the witness) not going to answer that. Certify it. I'm going to shut the deposition down if you don't go to your next question. Don't Joe me asshole ... you could gag a maggot off a meat wagon.

Followed by: "Come on ... quit talking. Ask the question. Nobody wants to socialize with you ... you don't know what you're doing. Obviously someone wrote out a long outline of stuff for you to ask. You have no concept of what you're doing."

And finally

"Q. If you're going to hand the complaint to him to coach him we are going to see the judge.

O. Just get your foul, odious body on the other side.

Q. Then don't show the witness any more ...

O. I'm giving the witness the complaint ...

Q. You're not entitled to coach the witness any further ... you're not entitled to ...

O. Don't use your little sheeny, Hebrew tricks on me, Epstein.

Q. Off the record ...

O. No, on the record.

Q. You son of a bitch.

A. Let's call a recess.

Q. Tell the Judge I called him a rotten son of a bitch for calling me a sheeny Hebrew and I want to go see the Judge right now".

In yet another stark example of lack of civility in the profession: the following is a discussion from a decision issued by an upstate New York judge concerning personal attacks leveled by one attorney against his unfortunate adversary.

The judge sets forth the statements made by the one attorney about the other as follows: "Mr. X avers that Mr. Y parrots Ms. R's bold-faced lie that it is not her signature that appears on the documents." "'Mr. Y's incompetence doesn't stop there ... Perhaps Mr. Y should be required, in the future, to annex a copy of his law school diploma along with proof that he is a member, in good standing of the New York Bar, and not the Bar that he must do his drinking in; the only explanation that I can think of to explain his profound level of incompetence ... Mr. Y better get himself a better lawyer than he is to defend him when I sue him for libel. It won't be hard to find a better lawyer than he is. Maybe he would like to hire my Swiss Mountain Dog, Clyde ... Clyde may not be admitted to practice in New York, and may not be a law school graduate, but he is better groomed. While he does bark, he does not growl or bite on command as apparently Mr. Y will do for Ms. R and he [Clyde] is very particular with respect to who he will take orders from; something that cannot be said about Mr. Y, who apparently will take his marching orders from anyone as evidenced by his representing Ms. R, a wacko if ever there was one. Wakeup, Mr. Y. "I was just taking orders", is a defense that went by the Boards at Neurenberg (sic). The lock-step has not been politically correct for a long time, Mr. Y, or are you, too busy counting your blood money to notice!!!

Perhaps Mr. Y would like to share which District Attorney's Office [is] currently conducting this investigation. Maybe it's the Gotham District Attorney's Office on the planet Hollywood. Hopefully, it is not the same staff that is searching either for Jimmy Hoffa … This fine attorney goes on to describe his unfortunate adversary as: "the same genius Robert 'Clarence Darrow' Mr. Y". He goes on to state: "Costs and sanctions!!! How much is too much to discourage Mr. Y and Ms. R from ever showing up in this Court again. $10,000.00 comes to mind and in the case of Mr. Y, referral to the Grievance Committee to save the human race seem necessary, since I assume that a firing squad may be deemed over-kill'".

Fortunately, this utter buffoon of an attorney was instead cautioned himself by the court for making such horrific statements about a fellow member of the Bar. Well done, court. Well done.

Another genius in Bronx County, New York has been suspended from the practice of law for "a pattern of misconduct involving sexually oriented or other offensive comments directed at female attorneys". This fine attorney in Court invited a female attorney to guess the bra size of a 14 year old client. He was also known to hand out candy peppermint balls to female attorneys in Court, asking if they wanted to "suck one of my balls?" On another occasion, this idiot announced as an overweight female attorney entered the courtroom: "Here is the elephant, she's coming in. Who wants tickets? Come see the show". Finally, he once referred to a female attorney as "pig vomit on my shoes".

The Crazed Attorney

One particularly hot day in the Westchester County, New York Supreme Court, an attorney handling a trial mentioned to the judge: "Your honor, it's kind of hot in here, don't you think?" The attorney turned several times to the jury and asked them the same sort of thing. The attorney then returned to his trial table and produced a pair of scissors from his litigation bag.[1] He then used the scissors to make himself an instant short-sleeve shirt: in the midst of the trial.

This same attorney, seeking to make the point to a city council that the council was causing more harm to the city than good, entered the council chambers with the same large bag. This time he produced a heavy set of chains; threw them down on the conference table, and told the council it was "keeping this city in chains!"

A client once brought me a letter sent to him by his former attorney, who was advising the client that he had decided to retire from the practice of law. The attorney lamented his deteriorating physical health and how his hands had become so involved with arthritis that he could no longer "hold a shapely female breast".

The Farting Lawyer

I was once brought into a law firm to discuss handling an appeal for the firm. I sat in a small conference room and awaited the arrival of the partner and his file, hoping that this might be a lucrative appeal for my firm. Appeals can be a good source of money. I did not end up taking on the appeal, but I did end up taking in a lot of gas, as the attorney unabashedly let out a continuous stream of loud farts during our entire half hour session. It's amazing how people can sit in a room with a giant elephant bounding around, yet nobody asks why there is an elephant bounding around the room.

The Paper Chase

A colleague once had a deposition with an insurance defense attorney where his adversary grabbed a document out of his hands and ran out of the room with it: prompting the other lawyer to run after him trying to get his document back. The chase continued throughout the law firm, with members of the defense firm cheering on the front runner, like an Olympic marathon racer.

---

1.   This is a gigantic, ugly box with a handle that looks like a door-to-door shoe salesman's bag.

The Annoying

One of the more particularly annoying types of adversaries is the one who feels the need to "try" the case at every contrived opportunity from the filing of suit up until the actual trial. I suppose these attorneys become rather burned out in the process since they usually end up falling far short of the mark by the time of the actual trial of the case. I handled a case against such an adversary recently. You could not call this attorney and ask for a convenient date to take a deposition without his launching into a fifteen minute diatribe about how his client had been wronged by your client, and how your client had committed perjury, and had filed a frivolous case, and the like. You couldn't even talk about sports or the weather without setting this lunatic off into another self-righteous tirade. At a recent court conference, for the routine purpose of setting dates for compliance with discovery, this attorney could not keep himself in his seat before the judge's law secretary, squirming and jumping out of his seat, leveling absurd accusations against my client, and against me. This attorney missed his calling in life. He should have joined the circus as some form of clown: the bald head (shaded blood red with rage), the eyes bulging through coke-bottle thick glasses, and the like. This is the law's version of "raging bullshit". After the usual fifteen minute ranting, the judge's law secretary asked me what my position was. I told the law secretary that my position did not really matter because if my adversary kept up the way he was going he would soon be dead from a stroke.

These types of attorneys are basically the same people who were once the law students who, immediately following an exam, would feel the need to educate the class on all their perceived correct answers to the exam questions. These were also the people who would walk away from the posting of grades with their heads bowed to the ground. They talk the talk, but they don't walk the walk. I must confess that dealing with this type of adversary can be even more annoying than dealing with the constant phone calling client.

I had the misfortune to handle a case several years earlier against another one of these self-righteous types. This attorney apparently had the same modus operandi for all of his adversaries. I suppose no one had ever filed a case against any of his clients with any shred of merit to it: or so he would have you believe. This attorney was fond of personal assaults on other attorneys. He would get so worked up, you would swear that the man was going to have a heart attack and die right on the spot. Well, guess what? He did. He is now arguing his cases before a higher court, and may God have more mercy on his sad excuse for a soul than he had on the people who had the misfortune to have dealt with him in this life.

A Bit of Slapstick Humor you won't see on Television: Television programs portray lawyers as extraordinarily well-dressed, coiffed, handsome[2] (or beautiful, as the gender goes) individuals who are well-spoken, always on the money with their arguments and highly aggressive. Television lawyers occupy huge, swank offices constructed of mahogany, marble, steel and glass. Television lawyers drive a Mercedes Benz, BMW or Porsche. Television lawyers never make mistakes and certainly are not subject to the everyday gaffes that the rest of society must endure. In reality, nothing could be further from the truth.[3]

I wish I had a dime for every time I got a flat tire on my way to court and found myself standing by the side of the road, jacking up my old Toyota Corolla and changing the tire in 90 degree weather. Cars always seem to break down in hot, sticky, humid weather, don't they? After getting my car back on the road, I would, of course, be late for court, drenched in sweat and covered with auto grease and grime. I once appeared in federal court where my adversary placed a pen in his shirt pocket, only to find out as he was appearing before the judge that

---

2.   I have been in this profession for twenty-one years and I have yet to see any male attorney who looked anything like Dylan McDermott or any female attorney who looked anything like Jeri Ryan.

3.   Each season, the lawyer television programs are becoming more and more divorced from reality. The new offerings include "Shark", with James Woods and "Justice" with Victor Garber. These attorneys exude a level of confidence and arrogance which could only be exhibited by a person who is an actor. Unlike lawyers, actors make tens of millions of dollars for their trade (once they have reached the pinnacle of their profession, as have James Woods and Victor Garber). Actors do not have to sit up all night worrying about the possibility of being sued for legal malpractice. Actors don't really have to stand up in front of vicious judges or try to keep track of the thousands of deadlines real lawyers must somehow keep stuffed inside their heads. Actors are always perfectly eloquent before the TV judge because if they make the slightest mistake, they can simply cut the filming, take ten, and do a re-take.

the pen had leaked blue ink all over his white shirt.[4] The judge pointed this out to him.

I have seen attorneys swagger up to the judge's bench with the usual false bravado, only to trip and fall squarely in front of the judge. I was trying a case in federal court with an 80 year old friend and colleague, when the judge asked the attorneys to approach the bench.[5] My colleague and I had set up our counsel table[6] with all of the papers and documents we needed to start the trial. My friend had placed his briefcase[7] slightly in front of the counsel table and then emptied its contents onto the table. When the judge asked us to approach, he jumped up, ran around the table and fell head over heels over the bag, with his hands straight out in front of him: like Superman flying through the air. Of course, it was everything I could do to keep from laughing.

A friend was once conducting a deposition.[8] The stenographer was using an electronic, computerized stenographic recording device. These devices are starting to replace the old stenographic machines one sees in Perry Mason re-runs. However, as a rule, the court system is usually one of the last hold-outs when it comes to accepting and adopting new technology. In any event, this deposition was taking place in a small room, where the attorneys, the witness and the stenog-

---

4. Not all attorneys employ the Mont Blanc pen. Most attorneys, being notoriously cheap, simply "take" pens from the stenographers' office when they hold depositions there. Stenographers are a wonderful source of free pens, paper clips, highlighters and the like. Sometimes they encourage the attorneys to take these items, for purposes of advertising, because the contact information of the stenographer is imprinted on these items. On other occasions, they do not encourage the outright theft of their office supplies.

5. "Approach" the bench, is a fancy way of saying "Come on up". The presiding judge sits behind a bench which is somewhat elevated from the rest of the courtroom. There are usually what are called counsel tables in between the gallery (where members of the public may sit when and if they have nothing better to do with their time) and the bench. The counsel tables are simply the tables where the attorneys may sit when they are actually handling a trial, or appearing before the judge in connection with some type of argument or application. There is a distance between the counsel tables and the bench which is sacrosanct territory. Nobody is allowed to trespass in this area, except the court stenographer and the court officers, that is, unless the judge invites the attorneys to "Approach".

6. See footnote above.

7. Actually, this is referred to as the "litigation bag". The litigation bag is an enormous, clumsy item which is most certainly the ugliest briefcase ever conceived of. It resembles a large rectangular box with a handle. You can always tell who is an attorney on the subway train: he's the guy lugging the litigation bag.

rapher were all cramped together. After several hours of questioning, the opposing/questioning attorney told my friend that he only had a few more questions and he suggested that a five minute break be taken for people to use the facilities, get a cup of coffee, and the like. Everyone got up and left the room. My friend, who was the last to leave the room, got up and promptly tripped over the wire leading from the power outlet to the stenographic machine. This shut down the stenographer's machine eliminating the entire deposition: every question posed and every answer given over an approximately 4 hour period.

Lawyer attire can be slap-stick humor in and of itself. One could write a book just about lawyer's attire and coiffure. I have had friends and colleagues bend over and split their pants in court, and then try to argue their case with one hand behind their back in an attempt to cover it up. I have had friends split their pants on the way to work and spend the entire day attempting to hide the fact that their underwear was showing: backing into elevators; staying glued to their office chair; walking backwards around the office and the like. The main reason why attorneys split their pants so often is that an attorney has so little time to exercise and eats out of frustration and anxiety, that the pants you purchased six months ago no longer fit you. Another reason is that attorneys usually can't justify buying new suits, after paying their own personal expenses and office expenses together with all the new court fees which keep increasing each year. Shoes are another sore spot. Just as attorneys must appear in court in a suit (female attorneys may wear a suit or appropriate dress), attorneys must also wear shoes. Sneakers in a courtroom simply cry out for the type of notice you don't want to have. In regard to shoes, I have stepped in puddles on rainy days outside of courthouses only to get that wet feeling under my feet. I then realized that I had holes in the bottom of my shoes. This has happened to several of my colleagues. Good shoes cost money. So does shoe repair.

The tailor-made Giorgio Armani suit worn by just about every television lawyer is rarely seen in the actual practice of law. Most attorneys simply try to get by with whatever is in their closet and still fits. The hope is that the other attorneys

---

8.   This is a pre-trial disclosure device whereby an attorney questions a witness (usually the opposing party in the case) under oath before a stenographer. The deposition usually takes place in the office of one of the attorneys representing a party to the case, or it can take place at the offices of the stenographer. Sometimes it takes place at the courthouse, which is a nightmare because of the horrific courthouse facilities for depositions. Some courts have strictly banned the taking of depositions at the courthouse because they either don't have the facilities or they simply do not want to be bothered with these things.

won't notice that you are wearing the same one or two suits over and over again. This usually isn't a problem as attorneys appear in different courts, before different judges and with different adversaries on a given day. It only becomes interesting when an attorney is handling a multi-day or multi-week trial. Judges could usually care less if an attorney wants to wear the same suit every day of a trial, but this is something jurors definitely notice.

Suits run the gamut. Most attorneys opt for the more traditional dark gray, lighter gray, dark blue or olive suit. However, some of the old-timers in the city courts wouldn't be caught dead in such outfits. They proudly parade around in the lime green suit, the lemon yellow suit, the orange or pumpkin-colored suit, and (my all-time favorite) the white with candy-stripe blue suit. They usually top this last one off with the large, white Panama hat. I doubt that you will ever see these suits on television.

Hair styles are another one of my favorite things. Some attorneys simply refuse to accept the fact that they are bald. I was forced to, so I finally started wearing alternately the marine-style crew cut and the shaved-head baldie. There are a lot of bald lawyers, very simply because the inordinate stress makes your hair fall out prematurely. Some lawyers will go to amazing lengths to put up the front of having hair. One attorney in Westchester County has almost no hair whatsoever on the top of his head, so he has grown the hair on the very back of his head down in long, blond tresses, half-way down to his shoulders. Other attorneys use what I refer to as the "Bronx or Brooklyn Comb-Over" technique. They have a little hair on one side of the head, so they grow it long and comb it all the way over to the other side. This makes for good sport when these guys go outside in a stiff breeze, and the wind pushes the hair straight up in the air, like a sail. Other attorneys use a more complex method of the comb-over technique. They take the remaining hair on their head and circle it around and around the bald areas of their head. This gives the appearance of a gyroscope. Other attorneys opt for hair transplantation. You can always tell the hair transplantation group because if you look closely enough you can see where the hair was simply inserted (or injected) into the bald areas. Also: with hair transplantation, the patient looks utterly horrific for several weeks following the procedure (you end up with little knots of hair jammed into your head). These attorneys try to schedule such procedures when they don't have to go to court, or when they are away on vacation. But, every so often one gets called into court unexpectedly. These attorneys usually wear a baseball hat (hopefully a team that is winning at the time) to and from the court. However, you can't wear the hat in the courtroom. Thus, the truth is revealed. The final groups are the attorneys who simply opt for the wig. Granted, there are some very good wigs on the market nowadays, such as the one Tommy Lee Jones wears when he shoots a film. However, you won't find these wigs in the court-room. The attorneys who wear these items opt for the old-fashioned, boot-black wigs, which stand several inches off the top of their head and have the appearance of nylon. These wigs are nothing shy of comical. They look like something an undertaker would glue to the head of a vain deceased man. You see more of them in the Bronx and in Brooklyn than anywhere else.

While on the subject of hair, some attorneys (and judges) must not take a very long look in the mirror in the morning. I recall having a case against an attorney who was described to me by a colleague as having "a veritable forest of ear hair". I thought he was exaggerating, until I met the attorney. You couldn't see his ears. It looked like he was wearing ear-muffs.[9] There is a judge in Kings County whom all the attorneys refer to as "Eyebrows Smith".[10] This judge's eyebrows are so thick and knotted together; it is difficult to concentrate on anything else when you appear before him. I recently finished a litigation against an attorney whose eyebrows were so long they curled downward from his face and hung over into his eyes. Hasn't this guy ever heard of a scissor?

I have a colleague in Connecticut who has the second largest moustache I have ever seen. He looks like an old western-style gunslinger, along the lines of Doc Holliday. The single largest moustache I have ever seen is sported by an attorney in Manhattan who looks like the movie critic Gene Shalit, except that his mous-tache spreads across his entire face, from ear to ear. It is gray and wild, and shoot-ing out in many directions. Other weird and wild hair styles include the almost-completely-bald older attorneys who sport the tiny pony-tail in the back (made up of the precious little hair they still have left). Another favorite is the Ron Kuby[11]-type attorney who has lots of hair and grows it down to the waistline (with or without pony-tail). I suppose these fellows are trying to make some sort of statement, although I don't know what the statement is. Lastly, we have attor-neys who insist on sporting wild, scraggily gray beards, as though this is supposed

---

9.   The Sharper Image (I understand this company was founded by an attorney) carries an ear and nose hair groomer. I can't for the life of me, understand why men don't use these tools. The way I figure things, it's bad enough that I am bald. I use one of these groomers every day.

10.   Okay, so I made up the surname "Smith". The nickname is accurate, though.

11.   This was the attorney who, together with William Kunstler, conjured up the prepos-terous "defense" of "Black Rage" as the justification for Colin Ferguson repeatedly firing, killing and wounding people on the Long Island Railroad in 1993. If ever there were a poster-child for capital punishment, it would be Colin Ferguson.

to be something attractive. We also have attorneys who sport the Millard Fillmore style sideburns. One is left with the impression that these attorneys either care not one iota for their personal appearance, or they believe that the "wild man" look serves them in the same manner as the Native Americans and Samoans utilized war paint: the wild look is supposed to frighten one's adversaries into submission.

12

Your own Lawyer: Friend or Foe?

When you, as a prospective client, approach an attorney for purposes of representation, as we discussed earlier, you generally have a problem. You most likely have a problem because you have an "enemy" of some form. The enemy can be someone you want to sue. It could be the guy who slammed his truck into the rear end of your compact car. The enemy may be the guy who is suing you, if you were the driver of the truck. The enemy may be the government which is trying to take your money by taxation, or trying to imprison you for some crime you supposedly committed. In any event, you are now safe because you are hiring an attorney. The relationship between you and your to-be-hired attorney is going to be like the old song: "It's you and me against the World". Well, think again. Many times, your own attorney can turn out to be more of a nightmare than the one you thought was your true enemy. We are talking about the nefarious Scheister Lawyer.

Honest Abe Krem[1]: Perhaps my all-time favorite scheister. We will refer to this scheister as "AK" for short. AK was asked to represent a client for the purpose of saving his restaurant business. The client was the owner of the property, and had leased out the restaurant to a tenant who was not paying the rent on time. As a result the client was falling behind in his own mortgage payments, taxes and the like on the rental property. The client's objective was to get the tenant current with the rent, and to get himself current with the mortgage holder and the outstanding taxes. This seems simple enough. If you are the attorney, you either make a deal with the existing tenant, or, if he proves that he cannot pay the rent, you throw him out and bring in someone who will pay the rent. This is not brain surgery. It's fairly easy stuff, particularly so outside of the five Boroughs of New York City. It's even easier with commercial, as opposed to residential, tenancies.

---

1. Obviously, the name has been changed to protect the guilty.

After about two or three years of so-called "representation", and legal bills in excess of $50,000.00, this was the end-result achieved by the attorney:

1. The tenant was out of the property;

2. The attorney himself was now the new tenant;

3. The attorney had a lease between himself and the client; and,

4. The lease provided, in essence, that the attorney could stay on as tenant for as long as he wanted, without having to pay rent, taxes or any other charges. The attorney was in the premises for life: free of charge.

As if the foregoing were not bad enough, the attorney obviously needed someone to run his restaurant since he had no idea whatsoever how to run such a business. Would you like to guess who ended up running the business? Let's review the facts. The client owns the property and he has a tenant renting out the restaurant. The tenant is somewhat behind in his rent. Now, after hiring the attorney, the client has a new tenant in place of the old tenant, but this new tenant has a contractual right not to pay rent. So the client is still not receiving any rent, *but now he has no legal right to receive rent.* Best of all, the client finds himself back in the kitchen of the restaurant cooking for the attorney's new customers. Any profit from the restaurant, of course, goes to the attorney, and the attorney is not only, not paying the client to run the restaurant, but he continues to run up the client's supposed legal bill to himself. This isn't the end of the story. The attorney needs more drones for his restaurant so he has the client bring the client's family members into the restaurant to help prepare and serve meals. None of these people get paid any wages either. It's still not the end of the story. The client's brother is in the restaurant supply business. Would you like to guess where the attorney obtains his supplies from? Would you also like to guess whether this guy was paid?

If the foregoing were not bad enough, our good friend and conniver, AK, manipulates another unrelated client and that client's wife into working at the restaurant: again with no wages whatsoever. AK convinces these people that they owe him thousands of dollars in supposed legal fees, and that the only way they can pay him is to work it off at the restaurant. If that isn't bad enough, he convinces them to "lend" him the only money they have in this World ($5,000.00 saved for their daughter's future college fund). Guess who doesn't pay the loan back?

I like to refer to this as the story of the Great Restaurant Caper: The Attorney who stole a restaurant from his client. It happens. And, worse things happen.

We are not done with our favorite character AK yet. Not content with the heist of the restaurant, he then sets his eyes on enslaving yet another client. Mr. Perkins comes to Honest Abe Krem with a landlord-tenant problem. Mr. Perkins is in the process of being evicted from the hovel of a home he is renting from another crazed attorney/landlord from California. The client advises his new attorney (AK) that the home is virtually unlivable. AK assures him not to worry about the eviction and that he will take care of everything, so long as the client pays him first. "I get paid first" insists our friend AK. Since the client has no income other than a disability pension, AK convinces him to have the pension checks sent directly to AK's office—"the checks will be safe here from your creditors". Of course, the law of the State of New York prevents creditors from reaching pension funds, but perhaps AK has overlooked this.

Over the course of many months, AK has managed to purloin the client's pension checks, depositing them into his own accounts and giving virtually nothing of this money to the client. If that isn't bad enough, AK manipulates the client into performing numerous jobs for him, including conducting investigations of adversaries, to the more mundane projects of walking AK's dog, taking out the garbage and the like.

The short end of the story is that the client was ultimately evicted because the attorney, despite charging thousands of dollars in legal fees, refused to appear in court to contest the eviction proceeding. The client ended up with a substantial monetary judgment entered against him as well. The client had a heart attack as a result of the stress from these events. He and his wife lived from run-down motel to motel, at one point living at a truck stop next door to an Indian restaurant where they had to endure the odor of curry twenty four hours a day. During most of this time, the client was duped into working as an investigator for the attorney, at the attorney's law office: you guessed it, for no pay. I refer to this one as the Great Pension Check Caper.

The story of Mr. Tinder: Mr. Tinder was involved in a very serious automobile accident, for which he hired an attorney to represent him in a personal injury lawsuit. The attorney worked the case in a good fashion and was within a matter of days of settling the case for a few dollars less than the full amount of the liability insurance policy covering the person responsible for the accident. The problem was that the injured man's wife just happened to be a patient of Abe Krem's wife, who was her therapist and counselor. Naturally, Krem's wife played her husband up as the finest attorney in the county, so the wife convinced her husband to fire the prior attorney and to hire Abe Krem. Abe Krem immediately met with the new clients and promised them the moon and the stars. He could supposedly obtain money for these people far in excess of the insurance policy covering the offending driver. He would sue anyone and everyone until justice was done. Thus, the clients signed the usual contingency fee retainer agreement, meaning that the clients pay no legal fee unless and until the attorney brings about a recovery. In the event of a recovery, the gross recovery is essentially split on a 2/3 to the client, 1/3 to the attorney basis.[2]

The next thing Abe Krem does is to send a letter, signed by the clients, to the prior attorneys notifying them that they have been terminated in favor of Krem. The very next day, Krem receives a facsimile letter from the prior attorneys advising that the insurance carrier for the offending driver has agreed to pay over its entire policy to settle the case. The facsimile is accompanied by a letter from the insurance carrier making the tender of the policy. The policy was for $100,000, and the attorneys would have been entitled to roughly $33,000 in fees. At this point in time, in accordance with the retainer agreement in effect between the clients (Mr. and Mrs. Tinder) and the prior attorney, and in accordance with New York law, the prior attorney is entitled to one third of the amount negotiated with the insurance carrier. But Abe Krem doesn't see it that way. He convinces the clients that they are being cheated, and that he can obtain more money directly from the offending driver and from the local government for the condition of the road upon which the accident occurred and against anyone who had anything vaguely to do with the accident. He convinces the clients to go ahead with the firing of their prior attorneys. The clients are sufficiently duped so that they join Krem in a lawsuit against their prior attorneys attempting to cut the prior attorneys out from any share of the settlement. This is after the prior attorneys did *all* the work in obtaining the perfectly acceptable settlement offer. Ultimately, Krem is able to negotiate a fee split with the prior attorneys, giving himself approximately $20,000.00 for doing essentially nothing.

But when the money arrives from the insurance carrier, Krem has another money-making scheme in mind. He has the clients sign a new Retainer Agreement, this time agreeing to give him the same contingency fee for filing suit against any other entity potentially responsible for the accident.[3] However, he also has the clients agree to pay him an hourly fee for him to "investigate" the circumstances surrounding the accident.

---

2.   The actual calculation is a bit more complicated than this, but the approximation is close enough for our purposes.

3.   This part of the agreement is simply redundant of the prior retainer agreement.

What Krem has done is to work out an illegal solution to the age-old problem of the contingency case. Every attorney wants to collect money at the end of a contingency case, but you may only do so legally if you collect money for the client. Here, we have a situation where Krem has himself set up to recover if the clients recover, but he can also bail out on the case if it ultimately turns out that he cannot recover, and he can get paid anyway. To make matters worse, he siphons the money off up-front from the settlement against the offending driver. Thus, when the smoke clears, out of the $100,000.00 settlement, the prior attorneys have $10,000.00; Abe Krem has $30,000.00; doctors and hospitals affording treatment to the injured person have most of the rest of the money; and the badly injured client is left with less than $5,000.00. Think it can't happen? It does.

Naturally, after spending approximately two years doing virtually nothing with the case—Abe even "refers" the case to another attorney to "investigate"—and then charges the client by the hour for his own review of the case as well as the other attorney's review—Abe decides not to continue with the case. By this time, the statute of limitations has expired as to any other persons who may have shared in the liability. So the client ends up in a far worse position than if he had simply stayed with the previous attorney. The attorney, on the other hand, makes $30,000 for doing nothing.

Mr. Tobacco

By far the most vicious supposed attorney I have run into during the course of my professional life is the nefarious Mr. Tobacco. Mr. Tobacco leaves Abe Krem in the dust when it comes to pure malice, and dogged mania. The tale of Mr. Tobacco and his client, Mr. Ventricle, in its shortened version, follows.

Mr. Ventricle was a full-time teacher/part-time carpenter who needed an attorney to represent him in connection with a divorce action filed against him by his wife of over twenty years. Mr. Ventricle's first attorney on the case (an arrogant, over-charging dwarf) had charged him close to ten thousand dollars for doing virtually nothing except provoking bitterness between Mr. Ventricle and his wife: feelings which were not present at the time she filed for the divorce. Mr. Ventricle's first attorney was a classic example of the Napoleonic Complex, this person being a tad shy of five feet tall, but with an ego taller than Yao Ming.[4]

It is a general principle that divorce attorneys are notoriously good at fomenting disputes between their respective clients. After all, if the clients have nothing to fight about and settle their divorce issues amicably, how are the attorneys going to make any money? No court appearances, no motions, no trials = no money. So rest assured, if you are not fighting with your spouse at the outset of the divorce, if the attorneys have any say in the matter, you will be tearing each other apart by the end.

In any event, Mr. Ventricle was referred to Mr. Tobacco as someone who understood these situations and someone who could really help him with his problems: someone who would be reasonable and not seek to fleece him. Someone who would try to resolve the dispute, not create additional ones. Mr. Ventricle hires Mr. Tobacco, and then the real fun begins.

Shortly after the hiring, Mr. Tobacco asked Mr. Ventricle to do some work around his home to "help him out" since Tobacco has "helped out" the client. Eventually, the small amount of work became a massive emergency project as the carpenter client discovered that his attorney's home was virtually ready to collapse due to faulty construction. As a result of the divorce proceeding, Ventricle is a broken man, both financially and emotionally. Nevertheless, he drops everything he is doing, including a couple of good paying carpentry jobs, and rushes to repair Mr. Tobacco's home. Mr. Tobacco works out an agreement with Mr. Ventricle whereby Ventricle must complete the entire job, including paying for all the materials himself, or ordering them on his own personal credit, and the only obligation Tobacco has is to pay Ventricle by the end of the Year, which is 7 months later. Can you imagine any contractor in a fairly-negotiated agreement signing on to a job like this? During the course of the project, Tobacco doesn't miss an opportunity to harass and annoy Ventricle while he is out working in the hot sun. Nor does he miss an opportunity to continually chisel down the price he had originally agreed to. Ultimately, Tobacco has re-negotiated the price down to the point where Ventricle is barely being reimbursed for the materials used, and

---

4.   Ego, in case you haven't already guessed it, is a big thing in the law. We have already discussed the various hair styles, wigs and the like. As another example of ego, lawyers feel compelled to drive expensive cars—the type of cars Wall Street executives can afford—even though the lawyers can't really afford them. This means that lawyers carry lots of debt. I personally know a number of lawyers who are so far behind the IRS in their tax payments they are on the verge of losing their homes to the government. I know another lawyer who has had the Sheriff show up at his home on several occasions to assess his assets for purposes of collecting a judgment against the attorney. I know another lawyer whose car was re-possessed in the middle of the night. The double-edged sword is that if you drive a really expensive car and act as though you are wealthy (when you aren't really wealthy) people will treat you that way. This means that when the plumber or electrician comes to an attorney's home to give an estimate, the attorney will always get a higher estimate than his next-door neighbor. This is yet another reason why I drive a Toyota Corolla. And, I never, ever tell a tradesperson that I am an attorney.

Ventricle has nothing paid toward his inordinate amount of time spent on the job.

When Ventricle comes within two days of completing the job, Tobacco shrewdly fires him at this point under a ruse, and has some cheap replacement worker finish the little of nothing needed to complete the project. At this point, Ventricle is out of pocket the materials and all of his labor for three months' work. And, it is now abundantly clear that Tobacco is not going to pay him one dime.

Ventricle is forced to file a mechanic's lien on Tobacco's home. This is the beginning of the mania. Any person in his right mind would settle up and be done with the matter. Not Tobacco. He rushes off to court—in order to get there first—and files a ridiculous lawsuit against Ventricle making all sorts of absurd claims in an effort to scare Ventricle into walking away from the money he is owed. But this isn't enough, Tobacco, who knows all along that Ventricle (a full-time teacher and part-time carpenter) has no licenses or registrations as a contractor, suddenly comes up with the revelation that he has been deceived by Ventricle into believing that Ventricle was, in fact, a licensed contractor. Tobacco, of course, knows that Ventricle is a part-time carpenter with no contractor's license because Tobacco is his attorney in the divorce action. Tobacco himself has made these very same arguments in the divorce action against Ventricle's wife. Based upon the newly-conjured defense of lack of contractor's license, and despite his written agreements and acknowledgement of the debt owed, he refuses to pay Ventricle one dime. This is a very obvious backwards rationalization to cheat Ventricle out of his hard-earned money. In other words, Tobacco has made himself a substantial windfall at his client's expense. He got his broken down house fixed by his client for free.

Even this isn't enough for the crooked Mr. Tobacco. Tobacco next files a complaint with the local Department of Consumer Affairs claiming again that he was deceived by Ventricle over the absurd licensing issue. Tobacco now makes litigation against his own client, Ventricle, his life's work. He is going to destroy every aspect of Ventricle's life if it's the last thing he ever does. He files frivolous motion, after frivolous motion, all in his scheme to get his job done for free, at the expense of his client. When all was said and done, he had managed to get the job done for free; tarnish Mr. Ventricle's name before his school employer; and, tarnish Mr. Ventricle's reputation as a carpenter as well.

As I stated above, sometimes your adversary can be less of an enemy than your own lawyer.

13

The law is a consuming profession

The time parameters vary with each attorney but a general rule of thumb is that lawyers have a tendency to become terribly out of shape anywhere between five to ten years into the profession. It's a given. When you spend fifty to sixty or more hours each week sitting at a desk, you are going to get fat. This has a great deal to do with the pants-splitting discussed earlier. Compound this with the statistic that approximately 50% of all trial lawyers abuse alcohol and/or drugs. That's a statistical fact. Add to this my pure observation only, that a good deal of trial attorneys also chain-smoke cigarettes (I once shared offices with a woman who smoked a minimum of three to four packs of cigarettes each day), and are substantially over-weight (I once had a case pending with an attorney who was at a minimum 500 pounds)[1] and you have all the ingredients for coronary by-pass surgery. Incidentally, this is yet another reason why physicians should be more friendly toward lawyers: with by-pass surgeries, intestinal disorders, psychiatric ailments, and substance abuse, attorneys are the medical community's best customers.

---

1. I recall two attorneys—each of whom weighed over three hundred pounds—trying a case involving heavy machinery (such as tractors and forklifts). The attorneys were joking in the courtroom hallway that they were so big they could serve as models, or exemplars, for the machinery.

14

A Profession of Integrity

I was handling a bank closing several years ago when it came time for me, as bank's closing counsel, to hold a small amount of money in escrow on behalf of the borrower. An "escrow" is a fancy term for an attorney holding something which does not belong to him or her. For obvious reasons, if an attorney is going to hold money or property in escrow, the property must be held in a place separate from the attorney's own money and property. The attorney essentially holds the property as a "Trustee". Believe it or not, the situation is not very different when you deposit money into your own bank account. You give the money over to the bank. Once you give over the money, you do not have it any longer. The bank is supposedly holding the money (or a credit in your favor) on your behalf. There is an element of trust that you will get your money back from the bank. To this day, even with the FDIC[1] and the FSLIC[2], there are still elderly people who would rather stuff mattresses with cash than give their money over to a bank: these people having given over their money to a bank many years ago just prior to the Great Depression and not having gotten it back.

Back to our closing: The borrower did not want to turn over this simple escrow of about $2,500.00, even after I assured him of the nature of the escrow, and the fact that there is in existence in the State of New York a Fund to protect the victims of escrow theft[3]. He told me that he had no particular reason to distrust me, but that he had given an escrow to his lawyer once before and that he had never received the money back. We attorneys are generally skeptical about such stories, but all doubt left me when he told me the name of the attorney he had given the money to. This poor guy had given his life savings to a disbarred

---

1. Federal Deposit Insurance Corporation.
2. Federal Savings and Loan Insurance Corporation.
3. This is the Lawyer Client Security Fund. Attorneys who don't steal from their clients must pay toward this fund set up to protect clients whose attorneys do steal from them.

attorney who is, to my knowledge, the New York State record-holder for stealing escrowed monies from clients. According to New York State records, this attorney stole tens of millions of dollars from clients in the course of his practice: that is before he was disbarred and arrested. He is serving a rather lengthy prison term even as we speak. Let us all hope he stays there. As for my closing, I worked out another arrangement for the borrower so that we did not need to take the escrow.

Recently, another distinguished member of the profession was indicted, this time for stealing more than $1.1 million from his clients. We are all familiar with the concept of a seller's attorney holding the contract deposit for the purchase of real estate in escrow. Sometimes the seller's attorney will also hold the entire sale proceeds, for a very short period of time, prior to disbursal to the client. It seems this particular attorney decided to hold the entire sale proceeds indefinitely. Another attorney in Lake Grove, New York was recently charged with stealing the entire proceeds of the sale of her 75 year old client's home, to wit, $230,000.00. This seems to be a modus operandi for a fair number of crooked attorneys. The Manhattan, New York District Attorney's Office is prosecuting an attorney for allegedly stealing $800,000.00 from real estate clients for, you guessed it, helping himself to the proceeds of the sale of his clients' (the sellers') respective homes. This attorney would continually pretend to postpone closing dates (after he had already closed the transactions and collected the sellers' proceeds of sale) thereby keeping his clients in the dark about the thefts.

In one of the largest single acts of theft, about three years ago, a Manhattan attorney was convicted of stealing $27.7 million from one client: a client which ended up in bankruptcy. Perhaps the client was bankrupted by its own attorney?

One of my favorite stories is that of the "Ten Point Men" from Long Island. You may have seen in the news several years ago a pack of decrepit, old men being led away in hand-cuffs in connection with an insurance scam which took place over many years in Long Island, New York. The Ten Point Men worked like this: you are the attorney handling a personal injury claim which is being adjusted (worked on for purposes of settlement or litigation) by the liability insurance company for the defendant. You have a "connection" at the insurance company. Let's say your claim is worth $45,000.00. You would rather make $75,000.00 because your legal fee would be $25,000.00, rather than $15,000.00 (for the $45,000.00 settlement). The ten point man can help. He works for the insurance company you are pursuing for a settlement. He will get authority from his superiors to pay out the $75,000.00, but he wants a kick-back of $7,500.00 (10% of the total settlement) from you. After the kick-back, you have netted a fee of $17,500.00, so you are still ahead of the game. When you start handling these cases in volume, the extra "lift" the ten point man gives you can add up to a lot of extra money. It is also extremely lucrative for the ten point man; that is unless he gets caught. How does he avoid getting caught? Simple: he has to document his claim file each step of the way to make it look like he has done the research and in his honest opinion the case is worth the higher figure. As you can imagine ten point men are difficult to catch, that is unless they get too greedy, and that is what happened to the old crooks from Long Island. These guys had been doing this sort of thing for many years. They got caught, I presume, when they started thinking about making some big hits just prior to retirement. It is fairly easy to sell your superiors on a $75,000.00 settlement as opposed to a $45,000.00 settlement. But how do you justify settling a claim everyone can see is worth no more than $30,000.00 for $200,000.00? That's when you get caught. That is what happened to the ten point men, and they are serving their respective sentences even as we speak.[4]

In yet another insurance fraud scheme, about three years ago three personal injury attorneys were charged, along with several employees of insurance brokerage firms, with allegedly selling information about automobile accident victims to middlemen who then steered the victims to clinics for unnecessary medical treatment. They also steered the victims to the attorneys to file phony claims. Two former police officers were part of the "steering" committee.

In another twist to the extent to which an attorney will go to get a lucrative personal injury case, an attorney was recently disbarred when she was caught participating in a scheme to bribe hospital workers for medical records to reveal candidates for personal injury lawsuits. Another personal injury attorney, this time from Manhattan, was recently arrested for allegedly doing the same thing.

This next tale falls into the category of whose money is it anyway? When an attorney settles a personal injury claim, the standard rule is that the attorney receives roughly one third of the settlement and the client receives two thirds of the settlement. Several years ago in the State of New York an attorney apparently thought he could improve on these percentages. He settled a case on behalf of the client for the sum of $100,000.00. He deposited the settlement funds into his trust account, and when the funds cleared, he paid himself—you guessed it—the full $100,000.00. It makes you wonder just how long the attorney thought he could put off his client's phone calls and inquiries before this theft came to light. The attorney was caught so red-handed that he did not contest the disbarment

---

4.   Two Staten Island attorneys were recently convicted of issuing payoffs to insurance claims adjustors, through middlemen, for favorable settlements.

proceedings or the larceny charges, and he is now thankfully out of the profession, and serving his prison sentence. This story was recently topped by the attorney who was charged with grand larceny for forging his client's signature to a release and then stealing the entire $160,000.00 settlement.[5] When repeatedly asked by the client where his money was, the attorney told the client that the settlement money was to be disbursed "periodically": Perhaps, once in a blue moon.

One can also steal money the slow and steady way. An attorney in New Jersey was recently indicted on charges that he "skimmed" money from the trust accounts of several clients, to the tune of $85,000.00. I suppose he thought if he took small amounts of money over a lengthy period of time perhaps the clients would not notice. He thought wrong.

A fertile ground for theft is in the area of theft from trusts. Individual clients aren't the only ones from whom money can be taken. A "Trust" is generally a legal fiction whereby money or property is held and administered on behalf of another person, living or deceased. A simple example of a trust is the bank account of a minor, which is held and administered by the guardian of the minor. Trusts are also set up for persons whose physical or mental disabilities call into question their ability to manage their own assets. Larger, more complex trusts involve massive holdings of real estate on behalf of limited partnerships, individuals and corporations. In any event, a Long Island City attorney was recently charged with stealing more than $1.2 million from the trusts of six incapacitated persons. These are persons who are utterly incapable of protecting themselves against such abuse. The attorney is basically given over the respective assets of the incapacitated person to pay out and administer for the good of the incapacitated person. Stealing money from these trusts is somewhat akin to taking candy from a baby: it's easy to do and particularly despicable.

In an unusual case of an attorney stealing from a trust, a Manhattan attorney was disbarred for stealing more than $500,000.00 from the trust of his own aunt, who was suffering from dementia and was confined to a nursing home. This fine former attorney's rationale for the theft was: "I knew it was wrong ... I did it because I wanted to maintain a certain lifestyle. I was fearful of what would happen to my marriage if I couldn't maintain that lifestyle".[6]

Think you need to own something in order to sell it? Think again. A disbarred attorney and his associate were recently charged by the Bronx County, New York

---

5. At least the attorney in the first scenario actually obtained a valid release signed by his client.
6. This "lifestyle" included owning a three bedroom Upper East Side, New York City condominium and other lavish personal expenses.

District Attorney's Office with allegedly selling a home without the owner's permission and attempting to sell yet another home using a false power of attorney and deed. Could you be selling your home today? Are you sure you're not?

Unfortunately, in addition to the outright thieves, there are some bona fide maniacs in the profession. Collection cases, for example, involve the attorney pursuing a claim on behalf of a client who is owed money by someone else. This is simple enough. The standard operating procedure is to send a claim letter, with the usual federally-mandated language in the case of a consumer debt.[7] If there is no response within the time allotted, the attorney files suit. A default judgment generally follows (except in the unusual case where the claim is contested), and then the attorney searches for assets of the defendant to seize. Collection cases are not brain surgery. Several years ago an attorney thought he could improve on the collection process. This attorney went to the place of business of the debtor (the person who owed the debt) along with his client, the creditor (the person to whom the debt was owed) in an attempt to "persuade" the debtor to pay up. The attorney apparently saw no particular problem, however, with bringing along his hand-gun. As he spoke to the debtor he had the gun in his hand, quite visible in his pocket, and made statements to the effect that "we have ways of making you pay" and the like. As you can imagine, this attorney is no longer a member of the legal profession. He may, however, be a member of the organized crime profession or is possibly residing in a psychiatric institution.

Another story from the "Married to the Mob" chronicles is that of the New York attorney who was recently indicted for allegedly conspiring with loan sharks to collect illegal loans. The accusation against the attorney alleges that he told a government informant that his clients had "broken the legs" of another borrower.

Falling into the above category is the indictment of a Scarsdale, New York attorney as part of a 30 year racketeering enterprise that included fraud, bribery, extortion and murder. The charges were issued against the Scarsdale attorney, who allegedly worked together in the scheme with a disbarred South Carolina attorney, who is serving a life sentence for murdering two individuals in connection with the enterprise.

Recently in the news I heard yet another amazing tale of integrity in the profession. It seems an attorney is in the process of being disbarred for—this is a great one—kidnapping his client and forcing her to work for him as a prostitute. I do not recall any particular ethical rule specifically dealing with kidnapping cli-

---

7.   If the debtor is a consumer, as opposed to a business organization, the provisions of the Fair Debt Collection Practices Act apply.

ents. Nor do I recall any specific rule advising an attorney not to pimp a client, but it would seem fairly obvious that this is not the type of attorney we really want in the profession.

Here's another one: the case of the lawyer who got his client coming and going. An attorney in upstate New York was recently disbarred for admittedly stealing money from his client, and then stealing money again from her estate after her death. Perhaps this attorney never heard the old adage that one should let the dead rest in peace.

One of the all-time great stories is that of the personal injury giant of Brooklyn who came toppling down several years ago. This attorney had gathered numerous other attorneys to himself and set up a fairly large firm consisting of various partners, associates, and investigators. The firm seemed to have a knack for attracting serious personal injury cases. As the venue[8] for most of these cases was the very plaintiff-friendly Kings County (Brooklyn), this firm was obtaining large, six-figure verdicts and good, solid settlements for its clientele. As you can imagine, a firm with so much success in so short a period of time started to attract the unwanted attention of the liability insurance carriers. Ultimately, a full-scale investigation of the firm was undertaken, including a United States Justice Department probe. The result was indictment, and conviction of the name partner of the firm, and numerous other partners, associates and employees of the firm.

Every attorney dreams of the "Great Case" walking into the office: the "Iron-Clad" case, where, for example, an obnoxious wealthy person from Scarsdale blows through a red traffic light (with plenty of witnesses standing around) running down with his Mercedes Benz, an unfortunate, minority person in the Bronx. The Scarsdale man has insurance coverage for several millions of dollars. The injured person, who just happened to have been thirty years of age with a high-paying job and in perfect health prior to the accident, is rendered permanently incapable of working and will spend the rest of his life in a wheelchair. As you can imagine, for most attorneys this fictional case never comes along.

Apparently, the Brooklyn firm discussed above managed to garner quite a few of these types of cases. But the government's investigation revealed that these cases were not falling into the firm's lap, so to speak. *Rather, the firm was manufacturing the cases.* For example, if a client came to the firm with an injury allegedly sustained in a parking lot, the firm's "investigators" (thugs, really) would go

---

8.   A complex word for the place (County) in which a case is filed and in which the trial will occur.

to the parking lot in the middle of the night and create the defect that the client supposedly tripped over. This means that these thugs would take a pick-axe out to the property and chop up the asphalt. In addition to this type of activity, the firm was also involved in falsifying automobile accidents. This firm was embroiled with fake clients, accidents which never happened and other mysteries. While this may all seem rather impossible, or of ancient history, it did indeed happen, and it all occurred within the 1980's and early 1990's. When one remembers that over ninety percent (90%) of all civil cases filed in court are settled prior to actual trial, such schemes can be accomplished. The attorneys as well as the non-attorneys from this law firm are currently serving their respective prison sentences.

And now, from the Timothy Leary side of the law we have the recent disbarment of an attorney who returned from Paris with over 21,000 tablets of the drug "Ecstasy" in his luggage. Apparently, this attorney was attempting to raise the profit level of his office with a bit of drug-dealing on the side. The end result is that he will be saving substantial monies on his living expenses as he becomes a ward of the state in prison.

In another drug related case, an attorney was recently sentenced to fourteen years in prison for arranging an exchange of military weapons for cocaine to supply a paramilitary group in South America.

The following are some other assorted examples of chicanery in the profession. All of the following cases are as reported in the New York Law Journal. The first one is straight out of an episode of "All in the Family", where Archie Bunker insists to Edith "Get me a Jew" for an attorney. An attorney in New York State was advertising to the Dominican community that his firm consisted of "Dominicans and Jews". In reality, his firm was not so composed. His rationale was that Jewish attorneys "are preferred over any other type of attorneys" in the Dominican community. End result: a six month suspension from practice.

Two Manhattan attorneys were recently convicted of mail fraud for switching retainer agreements on clients following the settlement of a case or verdict. One attorney also stole as much as $350,000.00 from clients in this manner. These attorneys would calculate the fee from a personal injury settlement at the conclusion of the case and then figure out which retainer agreement gave them the higher fee. They would then switch the retainer from a straight contingency fee (the attorney receives one third of the settlement) to a sliding scale fee[9] or vice-

---

9.   Still a contingency fee, but graded.

versa, depending upon which gave them the best result: An interesting twist to the time-honored bait and switch scheme.

The Bank Robber: A Long Island attorney was recently arrested and charged with stealing more than $700,000.00 from a mortgage banker. He managed to accumulate this amount of funds by embezzling from some 2,700 closings for the mortgage banker.

In the "No Good Deed Goes Unpunished" format is the tale of a Manhattan lawyer and his girlfriend who were arrested for heisting money from the September 11th Charity Fund set up to assist those who survived the attack on the Twin Towers in New York City on September 11, 2001. The woman claimed she had been forced out of her lower Manhattan apartment due to the terrorist strikes, when in reality she had vacated her apartment in order to effectuate repairs and she was residing in her other home in the wealthy, Long Island Hamptons (A very wealthy area in New York) on September 11th. The attorney had given his girlfriend an allegedly phony eviction notice and a phony job verification letter in support of the scam.

A court-appointed attorney found himself on the wrong end of a suspension when he attempted to charge an indigent client for representation. Under the rules of court appointments, the assigned counsel may not charge the indigent client. The Court system pays the attorney or the case must be handled on a Pro Bono Publico basis (meaning "For the Public Good", or without charge). In this case, the attorney told his client that he would receive "better representation" if the client paid him. Conclusively proving that you can't have your cake and eat it too, at least if the cake is being served by the government.

An attorney in Westchester County was recently disbarred from practice after having helped himself to almost three quarters of a million dollars in client trust funds, including money belonging to the County of Westchester and a municipality. The attorney had found himself in the position of the person writing checks for the municipality and the county. This means that the attorney held the checkbook for the county and the municipality and he had the right to issue these checks (obviously to persons other than himself). This is somewhat akin to permitting the lion to baby-sit for the lamb.

A Long Island, New York attorney was recently arrested and charged with stealing more than $1,000,000.00 from client escrow accounts, although the Nassau County District Attorney's Office is investigating figures as high as $4,000,000.00. This lawyer was transferred to a psychiatric hospital: probably a good place for most lawyers.

A Manhattan attorney was recently indicted for stealing $1.6 million from seven of his clients. He allegedly used the money, taken from client's escrow accounts, to pay for trips to the Caribbean, to buy a Lexus and BMW, for clothing and personal items (including Louis Vuitton). He also used the money to make payments to friends and relatives in the United States and Barbados. Some of his more endearing misdeeds included stealing $300,000.00 from two Barbadians who were the beneficiaries of their son's estate (their son had been stabbed to death in a shoplifting); stealing $450,000.00 from a trust established by a client who was dying of cancer; and, $69,000.00 taken from the proceeds of a life insurance policy that a woman left to her 17 year old son.

An attorney in Brooklyn recently resigned from the practice of law in utter disgrace and has pleaded guilty to fraud and forgery charges as a result of stealing more than $2 million from 20 elderly clients. The former attorney utilized a number of schemes including forging checks and setting up a mortgage investment scam. In one case, the attorney stole $600,000 from a 90 year old man by cashing in the man's life insurance policy, dipping into his bank account and selling the elderly gentleman's Miami apartment without his knowledge or consent. This guy gives thieves a bad name.

In the case of the High-Flying Attorney: a New York State bankruptcy attorney recently resigned from practice after admitting he had overcharged his clients about $51,000.00 worth of air travel expenses. He had been purchasing discount air travel tickets but charging his clients for the full fare.

In a similar case, a Manhattan attorney was recently publicly censured for falsifying an expense report arising out of a trip he took to Las Vegas, supposedly on client business. His reason for doing so: to cover up the fact that he had taken a "female companion" along with him. He had better hope that his wife does not read the New York Law Journal, where this story made the front page news.

The Manhattan District Attorney's Office very recently announced that two personal injury attorneys had pleaded guilty to stealing $275,000.00 from their clients by claiming bogus "expenses" in connection with personal injury claims. The two attorneys somehow managed to reach a figure of $275,000.00 by amassing small fake expenses ranging from $250.00 to $750.00 per client.

It was once said that fifty million Frenchmen can't be wrong. In this case, a New York attorney serving a prison sentence was disbarred for, among other things, submitting false Visa applications on behalf of 50 French hair-stylists seeking entry to the United States. What was this attorney planning to do with 50 French hair-stylists? I shudder to think.

This next situation involves the case of the Great Interceptor. A Queens attorney was recently disbarred for intercepting telephone messages left by clients for another law firm and then signing up these clients under the false assertion that the attorney had a relationship with the firm. The attorney would call the other law firm's answering service pretending to be a partner at the firm and then he would collect the other law firm's messages. He made a fair living intercepting the other firm's clients for a while: until he was caught (tackled, so to speak). Now that he is no longer practicing law, he should perhaps seek employment with the Oakland Raiders as a defensive back. The Raiders will sign just about anybody.

In the "Borrowing from Peter to pay Paul" category, we have the recent arrest of an attorney in Queens, New York for allegedly borrowing more than $60,000 from various clients' escrow accounts to loan to another client. The other client apparently never paid back the loan, leaving the attorney with a personal debt now owed to the escrow clients, as well as several charges of grand larceny and most likely disbarment. Thereby proving, that if you are going to steal the money you may as well steal it for yourself.

Who doesn't hate the IRS? A Westchester County, New York attorney, however, recently took matters a bit too far. He not only evaded his own personal taxes but also prepared false tax returns for a client of his accounting practice, and then obstructed an IRS investigation into the returns. After all that, it is rather ironic that the United States government will be paying his room and board for the next 5 years or so.

A Queens attorney was recently sanctioned for comments made about opposing counsel wherein he stated that his opposing counsel's style of practice: "indicates that she fits more as a clown in a circus than an attorney in a court of law". The Grievance Committee didn't clown around when it issued its decision sanctioning him.

The Lawyer who steals from other Lawyers (or from himself?): A New York City attorney recently resigned in utter disgrace after being caught stealing at least $110,000.00 in petty cash from the law firm in which he himself was a partner. Another attorney in Nassau County, New York was recently accused of stealing $500,000.00 from his own firm by writing out checks in the names of clients and depositing them into his own escrow account. The law firm issued the following statement immediately following the attorney's arrest: as soon as the attorney's "… activities came to light, his employment … was immediately terminated."

So far, we have been speaking mostly of the fine men of the legal profession. What about the female legal eagles? Recently, a young, female attorney was arrested when she visited her client at a prison in upstate New York. The client started out as the inmate. The attorney physically attacked several prison guards during the course of the visit, and she now shares the same fate as her client. Her license to practice law is also under review.

Not to be outdone in the violence category, an attorney was recently disbarred for murdering his ex-wife by shooting her and burying her body near a hiking trail in Maine. This sleazebag had denied the murder, attempting to blame it on his son and fiancé.

I recently heard a story on the news that caught my attention. It seems an attorney and his client were engaged in a dispute over a legal bill. The client adamantly refused to pay the bill, and the lawyer stood firm. This, in and of itself, is no revelation since this happens every day of the week. The point of interest was the manner in which the parties decided to "resolve" the dispute. They set a date for a boxing match at which the winner will either collect the fee, or drop the matter. Believe it or not this is not as novel an approach as one would think. It is actually a throw-back to the ancient days of "Trial by Combat" where a Knight or Champion would fight it out with his Challenger over a disputed issue. It is certainly a cheaper and faster alternative to today's expensive and dragged-out court process. The court system should perhaps look into this avenue of expedient dispute resolution. I, for one, would relish the thought of getting several judges into the ring.[10]

Another female attorney was recently disbarred following her conviction in a Florida federal court for using her trust account to launder money as part of an elaborate scheme to bilk a life insurance company out of $400,000.00. This resulted in the collapse of the life insurance company; so in essence, this attorney was greatly instrumental in bringing about the "death" of the life insurance company. The loss of her license to practice law is now the least of her concerns as she will be spending the next 24 years in a federal prison.

Here's another gem from the feminine side of the law. An attorney was recently disbarred for submitting a power of attorney to an insurance company—here's the punch line—one month *after the client who had signed the power of attorney died.* Apparently, the client must have signed the power of attorney from the grave. What is even more interesting is that the disbarment was based,

---

10. I have received a lot of criticism from my colleagues for not playing golf. I have been told flat out that I "must play golf" if I am to practice law. Personally, I can't think of anything more boring than the game of golf. And, how is someone supposed to stay in shape doing it? Instead, I study martial arts. I have been doing so off and on for 18 years.

in part, on the attorney's lying about the situation. This makes one wonder what exactly she lied about. She couldn't lie about the dates. It was fairly obvious when the client had died. Perhaps she sought to convince the court that the client was really alive after all: a twist on the "Weekend at Bernie's" defense. Not to be out-done, another female attorney was suspended from the bar for occupying her sis-ter's rent-regulated loft apartment in New York City. She indeed paid the rent. However, she paid the rent with checks bearing her sister's name. The trouble was that her sister couldn't have signed the checks since her sister had died.

A couple of years ago, a well-paid New York City female associate was sen-tenced to prison for stealing more than $110,000.00 from the law firm which employed her. She also set up an elaborate scheme with her boyfriend to bilk pro-spective investors out of their money. The victims of these schemes were prima-rily friends, relatives and co-workers, including the attorney's own personal secretary. The judge who sentenced this trash-bag stated in the course of the sen-tencing: "[T]here was no reason for this ... You weren't in need of money. All you were interested in was a very high lifestyle, living in the best hotels, [throw-ing] the best parties that everybody will go [to], spending other people's money".

A note about Lawyer Impersonators: As awful as it is to be an attorney it always amazes me that non-lawyers attempt to pass themselves off as one of us. Recently, a Florida resident was sentenced by a New York federal court for pass-ing himself off as an attorney and defrauding several law firms into paying him in excess of $200,000.00 in "legal fees". This enterprising chap would make tele-phone calls to major law firms nationwide. He would identify himself as a "part-ner" in a law firm and request the accounts payable managers of the firms to wire transfer money to his fictional law firm, from which he would then steal the money. He would convince the bookkeepers of these law firms that he was owed a debt by the firm. He banked on the assumption that these law firms are so large that the left hand sometimes doesn't know what the right hand is doing. This gentleman managed to pull the wool over the eyes of several of the largest, most prestigious law firms in the nation. Sounds like the film "Catch me if you can"?

Another very recent lawyer impersonation case came to an end when four members of a Staten Island, New York family pleaded guilty to cheating investors and homeowners out of $14 million in a variety of schemes through a fraudu-lently established law firm. This story is almost unbelievable, but unfortunately true. A husband and wife set up a fake "law firm" with their two sons: none of these persons was really an attorney. They used the "law firm" to steal money from various mortgage companies and for other fraudulent purposes.

Even the paralegals are in on the game: A former paralegal for a Long Island based company recently pleaded guilty to stealing $600,000.00 by creating bogus invoices from a law firm that worked for the company. The company issued the checks to the paralegal, which she deposited into an account she created, from which she stole the money.

Along these lines is a Suffolk County, New York woman who was recently sentenced to prison for collecting $32,000.00 in "legal fees" from eight "clients", when she was not admitted to practice law. This woman maintained a phony law practice in Astoria, Queens and in Patchogue, Long Island. In other words, this woman, who was not an attorney, actually maintained not one, but two, fake law offices.

The flip side of the coin is the attorney, who has either been disbarred from the practice of law or suspended from practice, but who insists on continuing to practice nonetheless. A disbarred Manhattan attorney was recently arrested and charged with continuing to practice law, after he was found to have been representing two criminal defendants in separate felony cases. Now, he is looking at defending himself in his own felony case. He had better hire a lawyer: one who is actually admitted to practice.

A disbarred Long Island attorney was recently charged with practicing law without a license. In the words of the Nassau County District Attorney's Office, this attorney continued to do business after his disbarment "as if nothing had changed". I have a hunch that things will soon be changing indeed for this former attorney as he faces up to 15 years in jail, if convicted.

An attorney in Syosset, New York, who continued to practice law for more than 11 years after having been disbarred, was recently sentenced to prison after being convicted of stealing over $600,000.00 from "clients" escrow accounts. Thus, this attorney not only continued to practice law after having lost his license, he continued to steal as well.

Another Long Island lawyer, already removed from the profession, was arrested for stealing roughly $77,000.00 from "clients". The money stolen was mostly in the form of down-payments clients thought they had been putting down on real estate they wished to purchase: thus bringing new meaning to the term "down-payment". The money went down alright. It went down into the disbarred attorney's pocket.

Another disbarred attorney was sentenced in Westchester County for continuing to act as an attorney and for continuing to swindle banks and individuals to the tune of over $1.2 million.

In the "You're never too old to steal" category, enter a Lake Ronkonkoma, New York husband and wife lawyer team. An 82 year old man and his almost 80 year old wife, each serving prison sentences, were recently denied parole under the following facts. At one time this dynamic duo were both marital partners and law partners, sharing a practice in Long Island, New York. During the course of their fine representation of clients, these two dipped into client escrow accounts in the early 1990's (when the couple were in their 70's) resulting in both attorneys losing their respective licenses to practice law, and convictions for grand larceny. The couple filed for bankruptcy, gave up all their property and were shipped off to their respective prisons. In the words of their attorney (who is also their daughter) "I won't tell you they are innocent ... the truth is they did a horrible, horrible thing and it was built on greed and some kind of pomposity.... Certainly my parents were very, very at fault.... They are criminals ... no question". Despite the foregoing, she nonetheless sought their early release from prison. As far as I can tell, the parents remain in prison to this day. With parents like these, it makes one wonder why someone would choose to follow in the same profession.

Another decrepit elderly attorney in Nassau County, New York was recently charged with embezzling $265,000.00 from various escrow accounts, including a refusal to produce a $63,000.00 escrow he had been holding for a real estate closing. The excuse for the alleged theft: a failing law practice, ailing health and the cost of his children's education. Anybody feel sorry for this guy? I don't.

Recently, a paralegal at a New York law firm was apparently out to prove that you don't need to be a full-fledged attorney to pull off a scam. This paralegal, it is alleged, stole the trial strategy of his firm, off the firm's computer, and attempted to sell it to the firm's adversary[11]. This guy is like the law's version of former FBI Agent Robert Hanssen. The silver lining to the cloud is that the authorities were tipped off by the opposing counsel, to whom the offer of sale was made. Perhaps there is hope for the profession.

A rather comical disbarment occurred several years ago, when a well-known matrimonial attorney pulled several stunts on his clients, including this one. The client, a woman, was about to go to trial on her divorce case, when the attorney accosted her outside the courtroom and told her that she had to pay him extra money, or else she was "on her own". In other words, he would not go forward with the trial. He managed to con the woman into giving over a valuable dia-

---

11.   This is sort of like the New Orleans Saints trying to steal the New England Patriots' playbook.

mond ring. But that was not enough. He insisted that she give him the ring, with the statement that she was doing so "for the highest quality legal services". The Ethics Board apparently disagreed and found the services to be low enough to justify disbarment.

In the "Ostrich with its head in the sand" category are two attorneys: one from New York and the other from Connecticut.

The Connecticut attorney was removed from the profession several years ago after failing to appear at court hearings, trials and depositions. He also failed to respond to client inquiries, failed to respond to adversaries' demands and generally failed to do anything whatsoever. An investigation of the attorney's office found unopened mail for approximately one year piled up in the attorney's office, as well as an answering machine which had apparently ceased taking messages after it became full many months previously.

Across the border in New York was an attorney who, after suspension from practice, turned over several files to another attorney, which files ultimately ended up on my desk. I found these files to be filled with unopened mail, unanswered messages from clients, statutes of limitations expired on cases, and generally nothing done.

Apparently, these last two attorneys believed that if they closed their eyes tightly, the whole thing would just go away. It doesn't.

Here's a tale about an attorney who apparently thought he was a judge. A prominent Long Island attorney was recently convicted for forging a federal magistrate's order and then lying about it to the government. The fake order purported to reverse a real order of the magistrate which had held against the attorney. The attorney hoped that the fake order would compel his adversary to settle the case. He was wrong. When the forged order came to light, the attorney arrogantly pretended to know nothing about it. This factor weighed heavily in favor of the prison sentence he was ultimately given.

In the "Fool Me Once, Fool Me Twice" category is the Manhattan attorney who was disbarred for stealing inside information from his law firm. He then embarked on a career as a stock broker, and was re-admitted to the bar.[12] The attorney has now found himself suspended from practice for a pattern of deception occurring during his period of disbarment.

What is it with lawyers and young girls? A 42 year old freak of a New York City tax attorney was very recently arrested on charges of rape and patronizing a

---

12.   This is a complex process which happens very infrequently. The usual rule is that once an attorney is disbarred, the profession has seen the last of him or her.

prostitute. He allegedly had been "renting" two girls, ages 15 and 13, from their mother. The married attorney had allegedly paid the mother's rent and "showered" her and her daughters with gifts and cash in return for sex. The attorney allegedly maintained an apartment in New York City to have his trysts with the young girls. He also allegedly paid the girls bribes to keep them quiet when authorities started to ask questions. He allegedly barraged the girls with telephone calls to keep them from turning him over to the police. He supposedly also gave the girls alcohol and marijuana as part of his sexual trysts. He was ultimately arrested near Toronto.

Not long ago, a 30 year old Long Island attorney was arrested for attempting to arrange a tryst with someone he believed to be a 13 year old girl: who turned out instead to be an undercover police officer. Another Long Island attorney (this time a 53 year old) was arrested and charged with arranging a tryst with someone he believed to be a 13 year old girl. This attorney was already facing federal bank fraud charges, and moments after his arraignment on the state charges involving the young girl, he was arrested again by the FBI on charges that he had violated his bail in connection with the federal fraud charges. And, finally another Long Island attorney was arrested and charged with attempting to disseminate indecent material to minors. This attorney allegedly had sexually explicit online conversations with an undercover agent posing as a 14 year old girl.

What about government attorneys? Have you ever appeared before a town or village board, or town council? If you have, you have most likely dealt with a town or village attorney. The town or village attorney is an attorney with a private practice who almost always knows someone in a level of authority at the town, such as the mayor, or chairperson of the reigning political party. The town attorney gets paid a small salary, but the position is generally a stepping stone to a judgeship or future mayoral position. These town attorneys have a lot of say about what gets done in town and what does not get done. One town attorney in downstate New York was recently sentenced for accepting bribes from a developer for pushing forward building and zoning applications for the developer's clients. This sort of thing most likely happens more frequently than we will ever know about since it is so difficult to catch such crooks.

One of my favorite town attorney stories is that of the Cocaine Cowboy from Westchester County. This eminent attorney got involved in drugs and theft, and then fled the country with his children's teenaged babysitter. Following his extradition from Israel, he was convicted and is now in prison with a lot of other cocaine addicts.

Not to be outdone by Westchester County, Rockland County now boasts a former town attorney who was recently sentenced to 15 months in prison for accepting bribes from a Rockland County developer to help push projects in his town.

In case you thought the nuttiness and criminal activity is confined to the members of the bar, think again. If one is looking for illegal and bizarre behavior from the judiciary, one need look no further than, Kings County, New York.

The recent conviction and disbarment of a Kings County judge, is at or near the top of the list. In most states, a case brought on behalf of an "infant" (generally someone under the age of 18) cannot be settled in the absence of judicial approval. Therefore, even if the plaintiff agrees to accept a certain amount of money in settlement of the case, and the defendant agrees to pay it, the case still may not be settled. A judge must determine whether the settlement is fair and just and in the best interest of the infant. In the case of this fine judge, the judge was looking out for his own interest rather than that of the child.

The judge allegedly strongly suggested to the plaintiff's attorney in private that he wanted $250,000.00 as a condition to his approving of the seven figure settlement. The rather shocked plaintiff's attorney instead paid a visit to the District Attorney, where he told his story and was then sent back to discuss the matter further with the judge: this time the attorney was wired with a microphone and recording device. Thus, the second time the judge in essence demanded the bribe money (note that the judge in a classic case of negotiating against oneself cut his demand to $115,000), he was caught on tape. This resulted, as one would expect, in quite a media outcry, as well as the disbarment and imprisonment of the judge. He sits in prison at this time, along with those he most likely sent there. Not a comforting thought if you're the judge.

In yet another Brooklyn scandal, a judge who has two other family members on the bench in the same court, was arrested on charges that he accepted bribes and favors for favorable rulings in matrimonial cases.

In the case of the afternoon delight judge, a Brooklyn hearing officer was recently fired for his handling of low-level violations such as disturbing the peace, carrying open liquor containers and the like. This judge would work a few hours in the morning and then take the rest of the day off. But, before he left for lunch, he would pre-sign orders dismissing cases and give these to his clerk to distribute later in the day.

Other Brooklyn judges have come under investigation for alleged nepotism in judicial appointments. Judicial appointments are one of the most lucrative areas of practice for politically connected lawyers. When a judge decides that a person is in need of a "Guardian" for his or her property (this person is called the "Ward"), the judge must appoint someone to administer the ward's assets. The guardian is virtually always, you guessed it, a local attorney who has managed to ingratiate himself with the judge making the appointment. These attorneys can be found working the political campaign contribution circuit, attending all of the political and societal dinners, golf outings and the like. Similarly, when a property or business is placed into "receivership" this means that the court, through the "Receiver", is essentially going to monitor the manner in which the business is operated. Who do you think the court is going to appoint the "Receiver"? You guessed it, the same politically active attorneys. Perhaps the single most nepotistic area of the law involves the New York Surrogates Court. This Court makes appointments of guardians, executors and trustees: all of whom are charged with administering the assets of other persons, alive or deceased. These trustees earn "Commissions" for handling the estates of their wards. As one can imagine, if the assets of the ward are substantial, the appointment can be very lucrative because the commissions to be earned by the attorneys can be staggering. The commissions are generally based upon the gross value of the estate. There is a very active market of attorneys courting Surrogates judges for these appointments. One would be a fool to believe that these Surrogates' appointments are given out on the basis of merit, or that they are given out at random.

Everyone in the legal profession knows that this is how business is transacted but the general public is intentionally kept in the dark. It may be in Brooklyn that this system of nepotism is finally being brought to light. Recently, the Commission on Judicial Conduct has been examining the system in—where else?—Kings County, New York. Several judges have been placed under investigation for irregularities in their appointments. This is the mere tip of the iceberg.

Nepotism and patronage are the name of the game in Brooklyn. At least five Brooklyn judges were recently notified that they are under investigation for irregularities, including failing to record the names of lawyers appointed by the court to manage properties under receivership. A two year investigation by a State Panel revealed "widespread irregularities" in the doling out of lucrative court appointments. What a surprise!

One judge in Brooklyn was recently admonished for essentially lobbying another judge on behalf of his friends. Yet another Brooklyn judge was censured for trying to influence a ruling involving a coop owned by the judge. Another Brooklyn judge was admonished for writing letters to a fellow judge requesting leniency for children of the first judge's clients.

The corruption never seems to end in Brooklyn. Yet another Brooklyn judge was recently convicted on charges that he accepted money and gifts in exchange for favorable rulings in matrimonial disputes. Also arraigned with the judge were an attorney, a businessman, a court officer and a former law clerk as well as three litigants. In this same court, in 1999 the chief clerk of the matrimonial part of the court had pleaded guilty to taking bribes over a seven year period for speeding cases along and for other favors.[13]

Recently, an upstate New York judge was recommended by the Commission on Judicial Conduct to be "censured" for threatening his estranged wife with a knife. Apparently, the judge had a few too many drinks one evening and held a carving knife to his wife's throat telling her he would "run [her] through" if she took his things without permission again. The criminal charges against the judge were ultimately dismissed, however, the ethics charges were, in the opinion of the Commission, proven sufficiently to invoke the censure. I question whether anyone would still want to appear before this particular judge, more or less be married to him?

Very recently an upstate New York justice was removed from the bench for having sex with a mentally retarded woman who had been placed under his care. This could be about as low as it gets, but who knows? Stay tuned.

Two upstate New York town justices should be removed from the bench, was the opinion of the State Commission on Judicial Conduct. Judge number one issued a search warrant for a car dealership and then turned around and called the dealership to warn it about the warrant. Judge number two apparently received money from an incarcerated business associate. The judge agreed to pay certain bills with the money but he never did, and then gave false testimony about the incident. Another upstate New York judge was censured for making repeated phone calls to another judge in order to secure the withdrawal of an order of protection issued against a friend of the censured judge. Yet another upstate New York judge was admonished for sending a letter, using the letterhead of the court, to his son's school challenging a determination of the school board. And, another judge was removed from the bench in upstate New York for misappropriating client funds as an attorney and then actively concealing the fraud.

On the lighter side of judicial misconduct were certain ridiculous comments made by a local judge in New York several years ago. Appearing before the judge on a misdemeanor charge of soliciting a prostitute (the defendant had hired a

13. The Brooklyn District Attorney's Office (the public prosecutor) is presently conducting an investigation into the claim that judgeships are "bought" in Brooklyn.

hooker) was a gentleman, who lived at a particular address at "John Street" within the community in which the case was pending. When given the defendant's address, the judge responded with something along the lines of: "John Street: That figures".

The "What could he possibly have been thinking" award must go to the local judge who took it upon himself to telephone a crime victim and try to convince her to drop her charges against a young man, where the charges were pending in that judge's court. If that were not enough, the judge had represented the father of the young man accused of the crime. It doesn't instill a lot of confidence in the impartiality of the judicial system when the judge is representing the father of the person you accuse, and he is trying to convince you to drop your case against the son.[14]

The New York State Commission on Judicial Conduct recently censured a judge for mocking the victim of an assault by comparing him to the lying "Saturday Night Live" character played by John Lovitz.

The New York State Commission on Judicial Conduct recently censured an upstate New York judge for, among other things, telling the town highway superintendent and a snowplow operator that if either of them ever appeared in his court, he would give them the "maximum sentence" the judge could impose. Apparently, the judge was upset over the way the snow on his street had been plowed.

Judges as Hired Guns: At least two judges have been removed from the bench for illegal possession of firearms, and one other judge has been reprimanded for firing his gun up in the air in a public area.

The Unabomber Judge: A former administrative judge was disbarred recently because he was convicted of reckless endangerment when he caused an explosion of an apartment building, as a result of his attempting to commit suicide. Hasn't this guy ever heard of sleeping pills?

Judicial Fatal Attraction: We also have the not one, but two, cases of stalking in New York perpetrated by the judges themselves. The first case involved a female judge from downstate New York who had apparently had a relationship with a co-equal judge in upstate New York. When the upstate judge apparently

---

14. This part-time judge has recently been removed from the bench for converting client funds as a private practitioner. His removal from the bench came 20 years after his brother was also removed as a Judge from the same court for making racists remarks and for other sundry transgressions. Like brother, like brother. It makes you wonder how intelligent the people in this locale could be if they elected the second judge after the removal from the bench of his brother.

sought to break off the relationship he was relentlessly stalked by the downstate judge, including many harassing telephone calls in the middle of the night and all that sort of good stuff. This case had the interesting twist where both the stalker and the stalked were sitting judges of the Court.

The second, more publicized case involved a stalking in upstate New York which was being very seriously investigated by the authorities. When the team of investigators finally put the pieces of the puzzle together they could hardly believe the direction in which they were headed. It appeared that the highest ranking judge in the State of New York was the most likely perpetrator of the crime. Indeed, as it turned out, the Chief Judge of New York's highest court was indeed the stalker. He was removed from the bench, and now, after serving his prison sentence, and blaming his actions on a psychiatric condition, he has actually managed to regain a fair degree of his former respect. He is currently touring the lecture circuit, for which I can assure you he earns more money than you do.

Very recently, an upstate New York City Court judge was censured (meaning, essentially this idiot was slapped on the wrist) for the following acts/comments: In one incident this Judge stepped down from the bench, disrobed and challenged a criminal defendant to a fist-fight. In another incident, this Judge suggested to police officers that they should "thump the shit out of" another supposedly disrespectfully individual. The Judge also approached a defendant and demanded: "You want a piece of me?"

The New York Times recently ran a front page article about the abuses of power in the lower courts in the State of New York. These would be the justice courts and, in some instances, city courts, mostly north of New York City. Some of the gems cited by the New York Times follow:

A Judge in one upstate court, who is a former state trooper with a high school diploma, refused to issue an order of protection in favor of a woman who claimed that her husband had choked her, kicked her in the stomach and threatened to kill her. The judge stated that: "Every woman needs a good pounding every now and then".

Another judge in Upstate New York (a boat hauler and high school graduate) when confronted with an African-American defendant being described as "that colored man", stated: "You know, I could understand if he [complaining witness] would have called you a Negro, or he had called you a nigger".

In yet another case of pre-judging, an Upstate New York judge made the following statement after arraigning three African-American defendants: "Oh it's been a rough day—all those blacks in here". A few years prior to that, a Catskill,

New York judge reminisced in court that it was safe for young women to walk around in his town "before the blacks and Puerto Ricans moved here."

A judge (a meat cutter by trade) in the Tupper Lake region of New York routinely jailed criminal defendants to coerce them into pleading guilty. He stated: "I'm almost like a pilot flying by the seat of my pants."

Another Upstate New York judge, who works for the telephone company, cursed at a defendant and jailed her without bail or a trial because she was having a feud with the judge over her dogs running loose.

One of my all-time favorite lines was that of a judge in Rockland County New York, who was arraigning a woman on charges that she had sexually abused a 12-year old boy, when he made the following statement: "Where were girls like you when I was 12?"[15]

And, now before we leave the court system, a word regarding the clerks of the court. In Kings County, New York a senior court clerk was arrested and charged with trafficking in marijuana, while on the job. Not to be outdone, a court officer in Queens County, New York was disciplined for stealing a superior's credit card and using it to call a phone sex number, while another court officer was punished for stealing narcotics being held as evidence in the court.

Finally, we score one for the law professors. A former copyright law professor was sentenced recently for having possession of 150,000 child pornography computer images. This genius actually downloaded the illegal images onto his computer at the law school where he had worked. This "gentleman" supposedly had the largest stash of child pornography ever found in Manhattan.

And thus we end our survey with one for the clients. A recent federal appeals court decision upheld the denial of trial counsel to a criminal defendant who punched out his defense attorney during the trial. Score one for the client: although he will have to celebrate his victory in prison.

---

15. The State of New York has finally formed a "Task Force" to address the problem with these local court justices, many of whom are non-attorneys. The Office of Court Administration has stated: "any suggestions from the bar association are welcome". I think the OCA will get a lot of suggestions.

15

Where do you want to be in the next 40 years?

The law is a fertile area for people who can't seem to retire. The courts in New York have probably seen more judges die while in office than retire. A judge in one of the courts in New York indeed passed away while on the bench. I wonder how long it took for the court officials to figure out that the Judge was indeed dead?[1]

The practice is littered with aging practitioners who can barely make their way up the courthouse steps. Hairpieces, false teeth and bad suits and ties abound. To see the worst dressed of the profession, go no further than Supreme Court, Bronx County. The lime green, banana yellow, striped blue and white and orange suit is still vogue in Bronx County. The Panama hat is also still in style there.

The talk around the courthouse is generally the same. Each attorney is still waiting for "The Big Case" to come in. You see the same long faces in the trial assignment parts day after day: The same insurance defense attorneys, the same plaintiff's attorneys. The plaintiff's attorneys await the one "Big Case" that is going to set them for retirement, and then if they ever actually get the one Big Case, they still don't retire. This is probably because after so many years of practicing law their spouses can't stand to have them around. I don't know what the defense attorneys hang around for. There is very little money in defense work because no client is cheaper than an insurance carrier. I suppose these people have no spouses to go home to: their spouses having all left for greener pastures.

It is a generally accepted fact that lawyers start to deteriorate from the stress of the profession anywhere between 15 to 20 years into the practice of law. If you

---

1. We attorneys usually refer to a judge who asks a lot of questions during an argument as a "Hot Bench". A judge who sits there and asks few or no questions is described as a "Cold Bench". I suppose the deceased judge would be the ultimate example of a Cold Bench.

went to law school directly from college, this would mean the average age of deterioration is between 39 and 45. The health gurus, such as Dr. Michael Roizen, tell us that your biological age (simply subtract your date of birth from the current date) is not as important as your "real age", which is determined by lifestyle, exercise, diet and generally how you feel about yourself. The trick is to have your "real age" be less than your biological age. In my opinion, attorneys routinely fail the "real age" test and come up a good deal older in "real age" than their contemporaries who have wisely chosen other professions.

On the subject of retirement: not only do lawyers fail or refuse to retire, but judges are notorious for refusing to retire. There are probably more senile and witless judges on the supposedly prestigious federal bench than anyone in the system would care to admit. Federal judges are, of course, appointed by the President of the United States with the "advice and consent of the Senate", which means basically that the President can appoint anyone he or she wants to the federal bench, as long as it doesn't ruffle the feathers of too many members of the opposing party. Furthermore, federal judges are appointed for life or "good behavior", which means basically that as long as the federal judge doesn't kill or rape someone (and get caught) he or she remains on the bench. In essence, once a federal judge takes the bench, no matter how stupid, senile, arrogant, inept or useless (sometimes all of the foregoing) the judge is, it is impossible to get this person off the bench.

While most state court judges are subject to mandatory retirement ages, usually ranging from the age of seventy to seventy-six, state court judges also seem to dread retirement and do anything they can to prolong their tenure. This might possibly have something to do with the fact that these judges are so used to people fawning all over them, day in, day out, that the thought of being home with their spouses, who most certainly will not be kissing their asses—is a thought more frightening than death itself. These judges keep retirement at bay by taking "senior" status, by becoming hearing officers, and in some instances working for private arbitration and mediation services. Anything, to stay away from their spouses, I suppose.

The attorneys in Brooklyn tell the tale of the judge who actually keeled over and died while on the bench.

In one of the New York counties we only recently saw the retirement of a judge who had presided over what used to be called the trial assignment part. It is now called the central calendar part. This is basically a cattle call, where all the attorneys whose cases are ready to be tried are called in to a large room—at the same time—and sorted out as to who gets a judge, who gets a jury and who gets neither and has to go home and come back another day. This judge started out as a tall, straight-backed, handsome gentleman with a strong voice and demeanor. Over the many years he had been on the bench, he graduated from the foregoing to a cane, then a four-point walker, to the point where he needed the walker and two strong court officers to carry him to the bench. From that point, he began holding court in a wheelchair. Had he not retired a few months ago, he most likely would have been holding court from a hospital bed or nursing facility. Actually, the functions performed by this judge could easily have been computerized. Furthermore, modern embalming and preserving techniques such as freeze-drying could have removed any obstacle to this judge remaining on the bench even after his death. One conjures up visions of the freeze-dried judge sitting on the bench, dressed in his robes, and parties appearing before him for assignment of their cases for trial. The attorneys would type the parameters of the case into a computer, which would randomly send the case out to trial, select a jury pool, send the case to another judge or adjourn the matter. I see no real impediment to this procedure. The parties would get exactly the kind of certainty that they came to court for in the first instance: pot luck.

You have to ask yourself, do I want to be staggering up a flight of steps wearing a bad hairpiece, with false teeth[2], and wearing a lime green suit, supported by a cane, or do I choose to enter some other profession and retire early? Do I want to be the guy meandering around the courthouse after his second bypass surgery, or would I prefer to be the guy calling him and pressuring him into having his next heart attack. The choice is yours. You can be the old man in the lime green suit, or the haggard old woman, or you can hire the old man in the lime green suit, from your Villa in Boca Raton.

You decide.

---

2.   Another ridiculous aspect of the television attorney is the way these people are portrayed as incredibly sexy, such as Jeri Ryan on the new television drama, "Shark". The producers of this show should come to court in Brooklyn, New York or the Bronx and see if they can find anyone who looks anything like Jeri Ryan. I have been practicing law in the courts of the States of New York and Connecticut for 21 years and I have yet to see any fellow attorney who looked anything like Jeri Ryan.

16

The Basic Problem with the Legal Profession is that it is an unnatural way to earn a living

The title of this final chapter pretty much says it all. The fundamental problem with the practice of law is that it is contrary to the natural way in which humankind was meant to live. That is, unless you believe, as Adolf Hitler did, that the natural state of humankind is war and conflict. I prefer the approach of the great teacher, philosopher, and leader, Mohandas Ghandi, who believed that the natural state of humankind is peaceful coexistence. Anything that strains against peaceful coexistence is against basic human nature, therefore, it results in unnatural stress and strain on the individual. Given time, this stress and strain wear the body and mind out.

Simply put, if you are in any way interested in law as a profession, you must ask yourself this basic question: do I want to spend the rest of my life fighting with people? If not, then don't become a lawyer because that is precisely what the practice of law is all about. There are admittedly certain areas of the law where the fighting is more pronounced and downright vicious than other areas of the law. At the top of this category is civil and criminal litigation. But, the basic concept of conflict pervades the entire profession.

Think about this for a moment. Nowhere in nature is there any relationship even approaching that of the lawyer/client relationship. Does a tiger need another tiger to negotiate itself a plea deal for the murder of a gazelle? Do monkeys need the service of other monkeys as attorneys to close a contract as to which pack of monkeys owns the exclusive rights to a particular tree? Do polar bears hire other polar bears as attorneys to work out territorial agreements amongst different families of bears? Clearly, lawyers are not needed in animal or plant societies.

What then is the basic purpose of lawyers in human society? Study some of the examples of the portrayal of lawyers in the Bible, which consists of the Torah, held sacred by the Jewish faith, and what is referred to as the "New Testament", held sacred by the Christian faith. On several occasions, lawyers try to entrap the person referred to as Jesus, who we all know to be a Jewish prophet living about two thousand years ago. That part is fact. The rest is belief, which we need not address here. On another occasion, a lawyer by the name of Tertullus tries to entrap the well-known Christian evangelist, Saint Paul. Each time, the lawyer is depicted as doing something negative. Is it a misperception, or perhaps is it because the lawyer *is* doing something negative?

What do we need lawyers for? In short, we need lawyers *only* because (1) people do bad things to other people; and, (2) people do not trust each other. Look at it in the reverse: if people didn't do bad things to each other, and people did trust each other, *we wouldn't need lawyers*. Thus, lawyers exist because of unnecessary negativity in human society. The entire premise of the profession is one of negativity.[1]

I'll prove my premise. The entire criminal law system is based upon people doing bad things to other people. We, as a society, need prosecutors (lawyers) to essentially separate the people who do the bad things from the people who were hurt by and potentially could be hurt by these bad people. We need defense attorneys (a lot of people would say we don't need defense attorneys) because, in theory, defense attorneys are supposed to ensure that people are not wrongfully labeled a "bad person", i.e., convicted, and separated from the society of good people. It makes sense that if a bad act has occurred, but the accused didn't commit it, then the accused should go free. In theory, defense attorneys exist to help ensure that good people aren't convicted of doing things that they didn't do. Many people would argue that defense attorneys also exist to "get criminals off", meaning that defense attorneys try to use what people refer to as "loopholes" in the law to free criminals. It is true that sometimes the law, in its zealous effort to

---

1.   In an Article entitled: "Emotional Distress and the Practice of Law", the Leading Causes of Lawyer Stress were listed, quite appropriately, as follows: "A. Stresses found Particularly in the Legal Profession: 1. Arising from the adversary system itself; 2. Arising from particular fields of practice; 3. Arising from conflicts based on one's role in the legal system." The Article goes on to state: "The adversary system itself can bring out negative behaviors such as hostility (the "Rambo litigator" syndrome), suspicion, manipulation and cynicism. These behaviors can lead to feelings of anger, fear, irritation and impatience." Excerpted from "The Institute for Continuing Legal Education", P.O. Box 30, Las Vegas, Nevada 89125-0030. Copyrighted material 1995. In short, as wise old Yoda would say, "The practice of law can lead to the Dark Side of the Force".

safeguard constitutional liberties, sometimes causes the unintended result that persons who indeed commit bad acts are indeed set free. But, this doesn't change the premise that lawyers exist because people do bad things to other people. Does it? In a perfect society, people wouldn't do bad things to other people, therefore the prosecutors and the defense attorneys would have no reason to exist, would they?

Next, the law exists because people don't trust each other. When purchasing a home, the buyer and seller must sign a contract and an attorney holds a deposit in escrow pending the closing. Both the buyer and the seller have an attorney. At the closing a deed is given from the seller to the buyer. In between the contracting and the closing, a search of title is made on behalf of the buyer. This is to check for mortgages, liens and other possible defects in the title to be purchased. If the buyer is borrowing money to make her purchase, she will have to sign a promissory note and a mortgage to a bank.

But why is the foregoing necessary? The contract of sale wouldn't be necessary if the buyer and seller simply agreed that the property would be transferred subject to a certain price, etc. If they trusted each other, there would be no need for the contract. The buyer wouldn't back out of the deal because she found a better buy somewhere else. And, the seller wouldn't back out of the deal because he found someone else he could sell the property to for more money. There would be no need to search title because the seller would give a truthful state of his title to the buyer, and that would be sufficient. There would be no need for a promissory note and mortgage to the bank because the buyer would simply agree to make payments to the bank, and the buyer would actually make the payments. Thus, if everyone trusted everyone else, and nobody cheated anybody, there would be no need for an attorney.[2]

The same can be said about the standard negligence action. If a driver were indeed at fault, he would admit his fault. A fair physical examination of the injured party would be held and a fair report generated. All parties would agree as

---

2.   One of the more comical aspects of the law is that lawyers are notorious for cheating each other, and for failing to pay their bills. Any court stenographer will regale you with his or her tales of how lawyers receive the results of the stenographer's work (a transcript of a hearing) and then try to stall out paying for the document for months and sometimes years. It is not at all unusual for lawyers to be sued by court stenographers and by other persons who provide services to the lawyers for their cases, such as expert witnesses and the like. The famous (or infamous) attorney, Roy Cohn, whom everyone thought was so wealthy due to the flamboyant lifestyle he led, reportedly left an estate owing substantial debts following his death.

to the nature and extent of the injuries sustained by the claimant and a fair settlement would be worked out. Again, we are assuming a level of trust, and that people want to treat each other fairly, i.e., people don't want to treat each other badly. Once again, no need for an attorney here.

I think the point has been made. If people could trust each other; did trust each other; and if people didn't hurt each other; the legal profession couldn't exist. It wouldn't need to. *Without conflict, lawyers simply do not exist.* [3]

The same cannot be said for other professions. We, as a society need architects, engineers and builders; that is, unless humankind would be satisfied living in stone-age conditions. We need housing. We need bridges. We need roads. Thus, we need architects, engineers and builders.

We need farmers, ranchers and fishermen. Without them, we starve. No more need be said about that.

We need physicians. Regardless of how you feel about chiropractors, osteopaths, naturopathic practitioners and the like, we need some form of medicine and those who can administer it. We get sick. We need physicians.

There are professions we don't necessarily need, but we find life rather droll without them. In this category would be professional athletes, actors, musicians and other artists. One way or the other, they perform a valuable function in our society, or at least most of them do.

With respect to the foregoing professions, do either of the two principles discussed above pertaining to lawyers apply? The answer is *no*. Even if we could (and did) trust each other, and even if people did not do bad things to each other, we would still need architects, engineers, builders, farmers, ranchers, fishermen and doctors. And, we would still want the entertainers. These people serve useful functions in and of themselves. They do not exist because of some negative element in society. And, this is what fundamentally sets lawyers apart from everybody else.

I then return to my original premises: the practice of law is an unnatural means of earning a living. It is an unnatural state of existence. You exist because of conflict. You become a part of the conflict. You are in a constant state of war. Many lawyers love to boast about their prowess in the practice of law. Some people boast about how "tough" their attorney is. What these people are really boasting about is their attorney's ability to wage war, his ability to survive conflict and to come out on top.

---

3.   There is an old story about the attorney who moved into a new town and set up shop, but he had no work, that is, until another attorney set up shop in the same town.

Here's the problem. Eventually, whether you are doing the hitting or whether someone is hitting you: you are still taking the hits. What better example than now-retired future hall of famer, Jerome Bettis, former running back for the Pittsburgh Steelers. No running back ever dished out the kind of punishment to would-be tacklers that Jerome Bettis did. People were shocked and even a bit disappointed when he retired. I wasn't. For every shot Bettis gave a defender, he got plenty of rock-solid shots in return. At the youthful age of 34, Jerome Bettis (the pounding running back) had himself been pounded. He retired after sustaining many injuries, and surgeries, with the desire to sustain no more. He's a smart guy. Tiki Barber former running back of the New York Giants also recently retired, at what would have seemed to have been the height of his career.[4] He too had had enough of the pounding.

Therefore, it doesn't matter how many victories you walk away from in court, one way or the other you are in a constant state of conflict, war and turmoil. Some lawyers brag that it doesn't affect them. They claim that they don't get "stressed out": stress and anxiety is for the other guy. They're dead wrong. Yes, the law is a very stressful profession. But, so is medicine. Perhaps even more so because the stakes are higher—someone could die. One could argue that stress is inherent in any manner of earning a living. That would be difficult to dispute. Even an author of children's books could find a publisher's demands and deadlines to be stressful. Coal mining, logging and fishing are particularly stressful professions because they are so physically dangerous. A lot of these people die on the job.

But to view the foregoing discussion to be about "stress" alone is overly simplistic. The fundamental problem with the practice of law—and those who practice it—is that the profession is enveloped in negativity. It is this constant negativity that saps the life energy out of lawyers and eventually leads to physical illness or mental illness[5], or worse. The worse are those who pretend to be immune to the stress and negativity[6] and end up living their lives as automatons.

---

4. Earl Campbell, the former star running back for the old Houston Oilers football team did not retire in a timely fashion. As a result, he can barely walk at the age of 52.

5. A colleague used to show up to work at the large law firm he was employed by with a brown paper bag to vomit into during the day because it made him sick just to be there. On several occasions, he was actually removed from the law firm by ambulance. Other stories surface regularly on the internet and in journals about attorneys crying on their way to work because they hate their jobs (and their employers) so much.

You simply cannot practice law and avoid conflict. And, conflict is the opposite of harmony.

As I stated above, if you are seriously considering law school, consider whether you want to spend the rest of your working life in a constant state of conflict, war, turmoil and negativity. If this is your cup of tea, by all means go on to law school with my blessing. But if you do not relish a life of constant conflict and turmoil, my advice is to avoid law school altogether. Keep your sanity. There are far better and more rewarding ways to earn a living and be happy while you are doing it.

---

6.   A good friend and colleague has spent his entire twenty-one year career denying that the law is a stressful profession. He has claimed that he "thrives" on it. He recently felt some chest pain and presented himself to his physician. Following exploratory surgery, it was found that his entire digestive system is ulcerated. He has ulcers all throughout the lining of his stomach and esophagus. He has kidney stones. He has blocked bile ducts. He is 45 years old.

APPENDIX

The following are some famous persons who made good life decisions for themselves[1]. They all had their encounters with the legal profession, but then thought better of it. As you will see, this was smart thinking on their part.

Monica Bellucci: It's only fair to start with the fairest of them all. The famous Italian actress and model, who has been voted sexiest woman alive several times, almost hid her astounding beauty from us all. Monica Bellucci actually started law school, but she needed money for tuition, so she began modeling to earn the money. The rest is history.

Maria Bello: the American beauty of an actress had every intention of becoming a lawyer. However, a little thing called acting got in the way.

Julio Iglesias: The famous singer and entertainer was indeed an attorney in his native country of Spain before he cast the profession aside in favor of, shall we say, other pursuits.

Geraldo Rivera: a 1969 graduate of Brooklyn Law School, in New York. Geraldo Rivera skipped out on the Courtroom scene, preferring the riches and fame of his present life.

Ruben Blades: This singer and actor was once an attorney in his native Panama: Yet another singer/entertainer who made the right decision.

John Cleese: In my opinion, the funniest man alive, this gentleman of Monty Python and Fawlty Towers fame, was enrolled in law school in his native Britain. I don't believe he finished as he got together with some other notorious sillies by the names of Graham Chapman, Eric Idle, Michael Palin, Terry Jones and Terry Gilliam instead, and the rest is gloriously hilarious history.

---

1. Stories are constantly surfacing about lawyers leaving the profession in droves. There are JD's (Juris Doctor: the degree awarded by law schools) spread throughout society employed in every conceivable line of work, other than the law. I am personally aware of two lawyers who left the profession to work for car dealerships. Other attorneys I am aware of have left to set up a cosmetic business; to work in a cosmetic business; to work in a health food store; to teach yoga; to own and operate a bed and breakfast; to own and operate a winery; and, to own and operate a laundry business.

John Grisham: This gentleman was actually a practicing lawyer (not a good thing) but he found a way out of the profession and became rich and famous in the process (a very, very good thing).

Ann Coulter: I suppose much the same can be said of Ann Coulter. This currently registered New York attorney is a firestorm of controversy, but she is also rich and famous.

Steve Young: The famous hall of fame former quarterback of the San Francisco 49'ers is an attorney. I do not know whether or not he practices. Let's hope for his sake he doesn't. One would think his compensation package from his former team, together with his broadcasting salary and plenty of lucrative endorsements would be enough to keep Steve out of the courtroom before he becomes as stressed-out as the rest of us.

Jennifer Lopez: The multi-talented J. Lo actually worked at a small Bronx law firm as a paralegal at one time: her parents having wanted her to become an attorney. Do we think she made the right decision in disregarding her parents' advice? I, unfortunately, listened to my parents' sage advice. She was smart enough not to. Instead, she followed her instincts and made her dream of becoming a star come true.

978-0-595-45231-6
0-595-45231-0

www.ingramcontent.com/pod-product-compliance
Lightning Source LLC
Chambersburg PA
CBHW030941180526
45163CB00002B/661